The ArchDaily Guide to Good Architecture

arch daily

gestalten

ON GIVING FORM TO THE PLACES WE LIVE

A foreword by Alejandro Aravena

Architecture is about giving form to the places where people live. It is no easier, and no more complicated, than that. There are three key words here: "form," "place," and "life." As soon as one reflects on these terms, one immediately comprehends that these things are not all that easy.

Let's start with place. Places can include private residences, social housing, schools, offices, shops, museums, palaces, government buildings, subway stations, bus stops, squares, parks, parking spaces, streets, the trees that line the streets (or don't), the sidewalks, the curb of the sidewalk ... I could go on. As an architect, this means that one has to be trained in the whole spectrum of programs that constitute our built environment, each of them requiring different logics, skills, agencies, scales, and sets of rules in order to deliver and perform properly.

Then, there is the question of form. What informs the form of a design? In architectural terms, society tends to think (and expect) that form is driven by aesthetics or the personal taste of a given designer. But creating a valuable design is far more complex than that—or should be. The forces an architect should be able to identify and address range from the concrete, measurable goals and objectives that one has to comply with—like building codes and regulations, budgets, deadlines, schedules, and similar constraints—to forces that may not have even been included in the original brief. For instance, the design's environment, its local pertinence, achieving the right orientation, the required physical resistance, or ensuring that it can be reasonably maintained. But in addition to these conventional forces, there are others that are harder to measure: an architect has to respond to aesthetics, but should also aim to contribute to the history of the discipline or the creation of a holistic design with an inherent cultural sensitivity. All of this different information affects the creative choices that must be made during the design process, resulting in a more—or less—successful form, depending on how each force is interpreted and addressed. A proper architectural response has to balance a sense of realism with the desire for something original.

Finally, it's a question of life. Buildings are ultimately designed to be inhabited, and are measured and tested by the unfolding of life itself. But what does it mean to live in a given building? The answer, once again, ranges from basic physical needs to the most intangible dimensions of the human condition; from being taken care of in a domesticated environment with reasonable levels of comfort, to addressing all kinds of symbolic and emotional responses that our surroundings inevitably trigger.

Another way of explaining this is through the lens of my mentor, the Chilean architect and academic Fernando Pérez Oyarzún, who, in his 1997 publication *El Espejo y el Manto (The Cloak and the Mirror)*, described architecture as being both a mirror and a cloak simultaneously. A "mirror," in the sense that, as a cultural object, the form of the places that people live in reflects society, history, a sensibility, a moment in time, and even the author of the design itself. Pérez uses the example of a window to explain good design. He says that if you pay attention to a window's height, dimensions, and the technology used to create its void, you could build an entire discourse: they are part of an architectural language, a word among a grammar, and as such, they are able to tell a story. If culturally interrogated, good architecture should be able to resist that intense scrutiny.

But, at the same time, a window's ultimate purpose is to completely disappear: to let in light and air, reveal a view. As a cloak, architecture should be able to shift from the foreground to the background, to completely disappear in the corner of one's eye, allowing and enabling people to simply live their lives. Good architecture, Pérez said, is always both things at the same time: a great cultural object that, if interrogated, reflects as many dimensions of reality as possible, but which simultaneously exists as a silent caretaker of people's lives.

Consequently, giving form to the places where people live is an endeavor that must tackle many fronts: from guaranteeing that all concrete, practical living standards are met, to interpreting and fulfilling human desires; from respecting the lone individual, to acting in service of the common good; and from efficiently hosting daily activities, to expanding the frontiers of civilization.

So, whoever makes an attempt first to root architecture in society, and then uses it to expand the possibilities of society, is on the right track in their efforts to make the discipline relevant. If your starting point is grounded in the wider world (rather than in architecture itself), and if you put your work to the test and measure its success within the context of the world-at-large, then there is a chance that architecture can be a valuable discipline for society—and not merely a costly one.

ARCHDAILY: A GLOBAL EXCHANGE

How a simple desire to share information sparked an international platform dedicated to democratizing architecture

Back in 2008, *ArchDaily* was born from a simple yet bold idea: to improve the quality of life in cities through shared information.

As architects, we understand that our journey is one of endless influences and constant learning, with everything that we see and experience feeding our creative minds. This well of knowledge and inspiration often lies dormant, awaiting the right moment, the right project to prompt a connection between divergent ideas, leading to a new solution. This inspiration comes from various sources: from our quotidian life, our interactions with the city and the environment, from books and media, or visits to remarkable works of architecture.

Having observed how the internet was democratizing the creation and proliferation of information, we saw an opportunity. What if architects had access to more information, better information? What if they could learn more closely from each other, and be exposed to more ideas? Could we scale inspiration? Could architects themselves do more, and do it better?

The fact that this project was started in Chile, far away from the usual global-network hubs, was actually one of its strengths. From our little corner of the world, we gained a very broad perspective on what was taking place in the world of architecture—from North America and Western Europe, to Latin America and the Global South. Our eyes were trained to seek out the unusual in architecture. We came to discover a fascinating new realm of structural design in places such as Paraguay, Ecuador, Vietnam, Indonesia, India, and Iran, among other destinations, where a new kind of architecture was brewing, catalyzed by necessity and resulting in a new expression of local cultures. We built a peer-to-peer network of architects across the world, bridging North, South, East, and West. To our delight, we began to witness the ways in which this collision of different contexts and ideas was sparking reciprocal nourishment, giving way to cross-pollination at an unprecedented speed.

That's the power of the internet and all that *ArchDaily* now embodies. Our mission to take our readers on a marvelous journey through architectural projects around the world has been embraced by architects and an ever-growing number of enthusiasts alike, all of whom make up the more than 17 million monthly visitors our platform now garners in 2022.

The sheer scale of *ArchDaily* now is a reflection of how important architecture is today, as the deepening complexity of our world places increasing pressure and demands upon our built environment. Architecture needs to scale, too, and for that, the availability and exchange of information and knowledge is crucial. To deal with issues such as the climate crisis, energy scarcity, population density, social inequality, housing shortages, fast-moving urbanization, diminished local identity, and a lack of diversity, architecture needs to open itself to the experience of other disciplines and diverse stakeholders. And in the process of opening, it in turn has the potential to influence other fields, from technology and interface design, to policy-making and social reform. In this gradual blurring of its boundaries, architecture is proving that it is no longer the domain of architects alone, and nor should it be.

As outlined by the Spanish architect and 1996 Pritzker Prize laureate Rafael Moneo, the current state of architecture is best viewed from the perspective of its evolution, dating back to the early dawn of civilization. "There was a time when building did not require the presence of an architect. The architect's trade had not yet made its appearance. Building was yet another activity among the many needed to survive," he said during his acceptance speech for the 2012 Prince of Asturias Award. "However, the necessary specialization that accompanied the evolution of the human species soon gave way to concrete tasks related to building that culminated in the appearance of the architect. It may well be the memory of that very remote past which is behind the instinct to build that still thrives within us today. The popular expression 'there is an architect inside every one of us,' would seem to confirm this."

That latent architect within each one of us is now waking up, and more and more people are beginning to care about architecture and wanting to be part of it. And just as the democratization of access, information, and tools has positively impacted various other industries, spanning retail, travel, healthcare, and finance, architecture might too reap the benefits of this ever-broadening world of exchange. From bits to atoms, from information to action.

In this new context, bolstered by our accumulated experience of curating more than 40,000 projects for *ArchDaily* over the past 15 years, we saw the opportunity to take pause. This book is a snapshot of the many facets of good architecture today. It considers the different ways in which the built environment is making an impact, and looks to convey this to a wider audience. As a guide, it seeks to unlock architecture's otherwise subjective nature, in a common language. In this way, we hope it will establish an informed dialogue between everybody who cares about architecture, who wants to engage with it on all kinds of different levels, be they architects or city-makers, politicians or community leaders, journalists or students, homeowners or anyone else besides.

Our responsibility lies with the built environment and with all its stakeholders, and that requires us to throw architecture's doors wide open. To define what good architecture is, in precise terms, is a challenge. Yet, through the introspective process of making a book, we hope to have encapsulated the spirit of *ArchDaily* over the years, foregrounding the architectural principles we hold in highest regard. The projects you will encounter here reflect a global community of world-shapers, marking the forefront of architectural thought and practice today. From visionary architects, emerging and established, to the topics and trends driving us towards a better built future, we are happy to share a cross section of some of the most inspiring innovators, ideas, and incredible feats of architecture that we've encountered thus far on our ongoing adventures in discovery and dialogue.

David Basulto,
Founder & Editor in Chief of ArchDaily

GOOD ARCHITECTURE IS CONSIDERATE

Considerate architecture is high quality, yet affordable, necessary, yet flexible, and nurturing of both people and planet

Besides denoting a show of careful thought, in architectural terms the word "considerate" also suggests an emotional and perhaps even empathetic approach. And why shouldn't it?

Good architecture should be considerate—in all the varied ways that word embodies. While it could start off with the motivation to do good, and require an initial moral approach, this sensibility, combined with a meticulous knowledge of individual/communal needs and transparent communication, generates a well-adapted, and accessible built environment that can promote growth.

Whether it shelters, facilitates work or a public service, brings people together, or reflects an idea through an aesthetic, good architecture is always purposeful. On the designer's part, this requires being attentive and open to all spatial, environmental, and human factors simultaneously. In order for buildings to serve meaningful roles in the lives of the individuals, groups, and communities that use them, the immediate and long-term requirements of these users must first be identified and addressed in the most respectful way possible. This also requires that this architecture be affordable, economically viable, and a response to necessity.

With the financial fluctuations of the global economy and growing wealth disparities in societies across the world, it is important for architects to engage their skills and knowledge to create a high-yet-attainable standard of living for everyone. This therefore involves devising an array of architectural typologies and innovative responses that mitigate construction costs and optimize utility. The financial benefits that a well-conceived and resourceful work can produce often in fact exceeds the price of its investment, both in terms of the project itself, and the social, environmental, and other external costs/implications caused by the development. Understanding the impact an architectural project can have is an essential part of the architect's primary study in the design stage.

This architectural principle also highlights the importance of designing with a site-specific outlook. A considerate approach does not waste valuable resources on a program that will not yield positive effects or be adopted and sustained by the people and place it's intended for. Often, the most successful outcomes occur when architectural interventions are based on societal involvement, ensuring a functional and sustainable result. A considerate project, whether built slowly or quickly, should be based on validated and frequent on-the-ground research. In addition, it should also involve the input of consultants, experts, and local crafts- and tradespeople, who can share their skills and knowledge to improve the development.

In our rapidly changing world, flexibility is also key to achieving truly considerate architecture, and many architects are devising smart solutions that render their work more adaptable and accommodating, for its current and its future users. This might mean that the nature of the project is one that is deliberately intended to evolve, like incremental housing, for instance, or else one that caters preemptively to a rapidly growing population. Flexibility can also extend to imbuing a building with multiple functions—a carpark that doubles as a playground for local children, for example, or a community center designed to bring people together, while simultaneously inspiring wonder through its majestic form.

Ultimately, a considerate project is one that is both supportive and nurturing—of people, of place, and of society. As evidenced in the diverse array of projects included in the following pages, it is a piece of infrastructure that is built because it is necessary, not simply because it can be built. And its intention is to generate sustainable, durable, and advantageous results that will improve and shape the lives of those that use it, both now and long into the future.

A GREEN OASIS FOR A SWARMING CITY

MIYASHITA PARK
NIKKEN SEKKEI
TOKYO, JAPAN

Miyashita Park cleverly responds to Japan's urban density with a public space catering to activity and relaxation. The park, designed by architects Nikken Sekkei, addresses the community's multiple needs by combining a park space—a treasured facility in urban Japan—with the public desire for a commercial hub, as well as a city-center hotel to attract visitors. "Miyashita Park is a project that raises issues from both the public and the commercial side about the ideal state of 'public space' in this new era," explains Nikken Sekkei.

The complex is an optimized reconstruction of the Shibuya Ward Miyashita Park, which opened in 1964 as a park set on top of a public parking lot. The new building addresses its predecessor's shortcomings, providing better accessibility, greater earthquake resistance in the increasingly quake-prone Tokyo, and enhanced amenities for the bustling commercial centers of Shibuya and Harajuku.

At 330 m long (1,083 ft), the elongated, four-story structure straddles intersections and sleekly embeds itself into the urban space. It runs partially adjacent to a busy train line and can easily be accessed by pedestrians via bridges and steps at various levels. Pathways lead foot traffic out of the concrete jungle and up to the rooftop park. To maximize urban greenery without the danger of trees falling on the nearby train tracks, a canopy was installed around the park's rooftop edge and the series of arched railings that hug the width of the building.

The commercial portion of the building includes a four-floor open-air mall that is "greener" in more ways than one. The outdoor walkways reduce energy consumption, removing the need to air-condition common areas, as in enclosed malls. By coincidence, the well-ventilated design has been immensely suited to the Covid-19 era. The indoor/outdoor restaurants allow diners the chance to enjoy the canopy and tree-lined Meiji-dori Street, with large sliding doors that provide the option of eating in or out. The 18-story hotel installed in the park—a first for Japan—maximizes both the utility and prosperity of the inner-city location. "The value this brings in terms of supporting the operational side of the park, as well as the community, thanks to the diverse array of visitors able to enjoy this unique 'park experience,' is something that could only have been possible through the framework of collaboration between public and private sectors, and the innovative design solutions this enabled," explains Nikkei Sekkai.

TOWER RECORDS

Miyashita Park's elongated four-story structure provides a new, spatially efficient model for mixed-use architecture in densely populated central Tokyo. As well as providing an elevated walkway and crossing (above), a lush, outdoor mall (opposite, top), and an enviably located multistory hotel, a sprawling rooftop park (opposite, bottom) provides the public with an essential green escape from the urban context, softening the presence of the busy train line that runs adjacent (previous page).

TOWER RECORDS
TOWER RECORDS

A BLUEPRINT FOR CARE, INSPIRED BY NATURE

MAGGIE'S YORKSHIRE
HEATHERWICK STUDIO
LEEDS, U.K.

Designed to reinvigorate, Maggie's Yorkshire provides holistic care to people with cancer. The charity was founded by the late Maggie Keswick Jencks, a writer, artist, and garden designer, who dedicated her time, following her terminal diagnosis, to creating uplifting cancer-care centers with access to plant life. Maggie's Yorkshire, based at St. James's University Hospital in Leeds, U.K., is designed by Heatherwick Studio, and is the charity's 26th facility.

The project takes inspiration from nature, with care its ultimate aim. "Drawing upon the belief that great design can help people feel better, Maggie's Yorkshire uses several 'healthy' materials and energy-saving techniques," explain the architects. The structure is made from prefabricated, sustainably sourced spruce timber. To ensure thermal efficiency, the building was designed with inbuilt passive ventilation provided by its form and orientation, and the use of porous materials, such as lime plaster.

Maggie's Yorkshire is awash with uplifting flora, inside and out, building up to the *pièce de résistance* on the roof. "The rooftop garden, created by landscape award-winning designers Balston Agius, is inspired by Yorkshire woodlands and features native-English species of plants, alongside areas of evergreen to provide warmth in the winter months," say the architects. "Inspired by Maggie Keswick Jencks's love of gardening, visitors are encouraged to participate in the care of the 23,000 bulbs and 17,000 plants on site."

Inside, the soft, rounded spaces undulate calmly into each other, creating a layout that is at once social and private, open-plan and enveloping. The center is made up of three large-scale planter structures. At the heart of each is a counseling room, surrounded by further amenities such as a central kitchen, and social spaces. There are windowsills and shelves, where visitors can place items from home, and large communal tables. "The interior of the center explores everything that is often missed in healing environments: natural and tactile materials, soft lighting, and a variety of spaces designed to encourage social opportunities as well as quiet contemplation," say the architects.

Maggie's Yorkshire's design embodies the charity's mission to provide holistic care within uplifting spaces. The site is home to tens of thousands of plants, including a bountiful rooftop garden (page 20 and opposite page, top) that connects to nature and invites gentle activity. Glazing floods the interior with natural light, bringing warmth into the cozy embrace of the timber structure (page 21), which houses communal spaces, therapy rooms, and private nooks (above and opposite, bottom).

AN URBAN LIVING ROOM FOR A GROWING COMMUNITY

GREEN SQUARE LIBRARY AND PLAZA

STUDIO HOLLENSTEIN

MELBOURNE, AUSTRALIA

Green Square Library and Plaza acts as an inviting "urban-living room" for the community of a newly developed Sydney neighborhood. The urban renewal project for Green Square Town Center is part of the Sustainable Sydney 2030 initiative, and is located outside of the city's inner suburbs, near to the international gateways of Port Botany and Sydney Airport. In 2012, a global architectural design competition was launched to find a sustainable, inclusive, and characterful public plaza and library to anchor the town.

The commission was won by Sydney-based architecture and urban design practice Studio Hollenstein, who planned a 3,000 m² (32,291 ft²) library, placed largely underground in order to maximize 8,000 m² (86,111 ft²) of open space in the plaza. "This arrangement allows the community to gather outdoors and enjoy the pleasant Sydney climate, while providing a community haven below with 42 large skylights delivering light to the space, where visitors can retreat from the noise of the city," explains Studio Hollenstein. Playful geometric elements of the single-floor library emerge into the open plaza space in the form of a pyramid, rectangular tower, and circular window.

The inviting library contains various community facilities including brightly colored meeting rooms, a computer laboratory, a music room (both for practice and performance), spacious reading rooms, a children's area, and an outdoor amphitheater. "The design is intentionally informal and programmatically sustainable, providing a shared territory for multiple uses—suitable for the evolving role of the library and an expanding population," explain the architects. The building delivers on sustainability, too—it was awarded a five-star rating from the Green Building Council of Australia—and boasts a central wastewater system and an energy-efficient ventilation scheme, which is cleverly fitted into the library's bookshelves. The underground structure's position on the water table also required the implementation of a secure, three-layer waterproofing strategy.

It is projected that by 2033, Green Square Town Center will be home to some 60,000 people. The plaza's intentionally sweeping, future-facing design is therefore ready to respond to this challenge. "[It] is a bold and generous space that will be actively shaped and remade by an evolving community," explain the architects. "This design makes space and preserves the plaza for community expression."

LIBRARY
-noun.
CAFENOUN

GREEN SQUARE
LIBRARY AND PLAZA

Green Square Library and Plaza provides the community of a newly developed Sydney town with a cultural and social center. The architectural program includes a generous square in which to enjoy Sydney's balmy climate, and a sprawling, light-flooded underground library with community facilities (opposite) that connects to the street-level plaza via a series of aesthetically pleasing geometric glass structures (previous page and above).

SOCIAL HOUSING FOR BUILDING BRIGHTER FUTURES

QUINTA MONROY

ELEMENTAL

IQUIQUE, CHILE

Quinta Monroy (also known as Incremental Housing) is a flexible social housing project designed to increase in value over time. The 2003 project was commissioned by the Chilean government to permanently settle 100 families living in a slum in the center of the desert town Iquique. It was taken on by Elemental, an architecture studio specializing in social housing. The practice was required to comply with the housing policy of the time, using the subsidy of just $7,500 USD per home to pay for the land, infrastructure, and architecture. At the time, the budget only allowed, on average, for a built space of roughly 30 m² (322 ft²).

To create housing that would provide for the families today and tomorrow, Elemental planned economically. "We have identified a set of design conditions through which a housing unit can increase its value over time without having to increase the amount of money of the current subsidy," explain the architects. A guiding focus of the project was to keep the inhabitants in their central location with its potential for increased property value. As such, instead of building on a larger piece of land in a cheaper, peripheral area, Elemental built a complex of architecturally solid "half houses" in situ in central Iquique. Made up of a ground and first floor, and fitted with the necessary amenities, these allowed 100 families to be comfortably housed, connected by a social, outdoor space. These homes, in their initial form, looked like a row of widely spaced townhouses, a deliberate tactic to encourage self-builds. Over time, families would be provided the technical support to expand the houses laterally, as needed, without sacrificing light, ventilation, or privacy, and the inner spaces have since been filled with colorful extensions and balconies.

With their housing model, Elemental encourages the state to rethink social housing as an investment rather than an expense. The architects argue that, for families receiving the housing subsidy in a central location, a house with the potential to grow could be "the key turning point to leaving poverty."

IN A PARKING LOT, FUNCTION MEETS FANTASY

PARK 'N' PLAY
JAJA ARCHITECTS
COPENHAGEN, DENMARK

Park 'n' Play reimagines the traditional, single-use parking lot as a space for wider community benefit with a living-green facade and playground rooftop. The Copenhagen building was commissioned as part of an urban-development plan to transform the former-industrial quarter of Nordhavn into a neighborhood district. To this end, a competition was launched for a carpark with a green facade that could engage broader public use. JAJA Architects produced the winning design, which, as they describe, sought to challenge the typology of the parking lot structure by providing the public with an "attractive public space" that could equally respect "the scale, history, and future urban culture of the new development" of Nordhavn.

The result is a building that merges the traditional parking-lot form with references to the district's origins and contemporary flair. The building is located in what is known as the Red Neighborhood, named for the traditional red-brick harbor buildings that punctuate Nordhavn. JAJA paid homage to the setting by coloring the building's boxy and industrial concrete structure an ochre-red hue to blend in with the surrounding red-tiled roofs and brick facades. The color has the dual effect of adding much-needed warmth to the notoriously drab disposition of the traditional parking lot.

Rather than cloaking the entire structure in vertical gardens, the architects chose a mixed-material approach. "Instead of concealing the parking structure, we proposed a concept that enhances the beauty of the structural grid while breaking up the scale of the massive facade," JAJA explains. Plant boxes are distributed rhythmically across the grid, adding organic volume to the exterior, while two large, public stairways provide access to the rooftop.

The stairs' playful, jagged forms, accentuated by their continuous bright red railing, lend the structure a striking dynamism, an element the architects say was inspired by the iconic, facade-sweeping stairways of the Centre Pompidou in Paris. On the rooftop, the playground is no less eye-catching. Employing the same cherry-red steel tubing as the stairwell railings, the shapely design incorporates swings, ball cages, and a jungle gym, as well as fencing and plants that arrange the space and protect against the weather. "From street level, the railing literally takes the visitors by the hand, inviting them on a trip to the rooftop landscape and amazing view of Copenhagen harbor," explains JAJA.

Park 'n' Play is a bold structure designed to equip a former-industrial residential district with both a parking lot and public playground. The ochre-red structure references Nordhavn's traditional red-brick masonry (previous page, left), and is punctuated with planters cascading with greenery (opposite, left). An exterior staircase (page 31, bottom) leads residents up to a generous rooftop playground with expansive views of Copenhagen (above).

REMOTE OUTPOSTS OF WONDER

PEACH HUT COMMUNITY CENTER

ATELIER XI

JIAOZUO, CHINA

Peach Hut Community Center is the first in a series of satellite community facilities being built to enrich the rural county of Xiuwu in China's Henan province. The project was originally commissioned as a 300 m² (3,229 ft²) public building to facilitate culture and art education for those living in the impoverished area. To better provide for locals living in villages spread out across the county, architects at Atelier Xi proposed dividing the project into smaller, cast-in-place concrete pavilions—a smarter, more considerate solution.

In remote areas such as this, "insufficient educational resources, inadequate information access, and scant aesthetic imagination" are commonplace, explains Atelier Xi. The facilities are designed as tree-shaped spaces reaching upwards, and play with light and shadow. They aim to enrich local life, beyond their practical use, with their visually stimulating forms. "The project aims to inspire the sensibilities of local residents, to help them enjoy and rethink life quality, as well as to alleviate isolation and poverty." The pavilions, which will also include a theater and library, will be placed in varying sites, from fields and woods to mountaintops, taking inspiration from their surroundings.

The Peach Hut Community Center, the inaugural building, stands in the middle of a peach orchard in Xiuwu. The sculptural 55 m² (592 ft²) structure is in dialogue with its environment, made of cherry-blossom pink cast-in-place concrete. The building and its curved entrance even lean to one side, echoing the peach trees' stoop. Using clever geometry, the building offers space for wonder, play, and education. On the second floor, a floor-to-ceiling window allows panoramic views over the treetops, while the structure's vertical corner windows provide a snapshot of the village from afar. The building is illuminated by skylights and a round window on the south side captures the ever-changing vista of the orchards in the day's light.

PEACH HUT COMMUNITY CENTER

Peach Hut Community Center is designed to bring joy to a remote community in China's Henan Province. Set in a vast peach orchard (opposite), the cast-in-concrete structure is inspired by the outward-branching form of a tree (page 34, top) and is colored a warm, dusty peach. Large windows frame the landscape (page 35 and opposite, top) while the day's changing light bounces off the playful geometry of the warm interior (opposite, below).

GOOD ARCHITECTURE IS DURABLE

Designed to outlast those that built it, durable architecture is strong in form, timeless in aesthetic, and dynamic in function

A durable building is not supposed simply to endure the passing of time, surpassing its expected lifespan or those of its neighboring constructions. Designing with durability in mind means understanding the building as a highly complex system that requires a systemic approach to the design process.

Given that constructing a building is a huge investment, both economically, environmentally, and in terms of energy expenditure, these vast costs must be justified. As the lifespan of a building becomes longer, it will have a more extended period of time to amortize the costs incurred in building it. Also, longer lifespans are beneficial to the environment, as the majority of energy consumption occurs pre-use in relation to resource extraction and manufacturing phases. Using a building for a longer period of time means lowering the annual share of embodied energy used for its construction. Plus, the more durable the architecture is, the less construction and demolition waste is created, which is one of the most fundamental architectural dilemmas of our time.

The resilience of the construction elements used and the need for structural integrity are important considerations when it comes to architecture being able to resist degradation, given that there are a wide range of factors that can weather a building and contribute to its decay. Decisions such as site, materials, form, and construction methods are all part of the detailed planning process required in order to achieve the best possible architectural outcome: namely, a building that is able to withstand the cumulative effects of environmental and time-related wear and tear, pressure or damage. Every building component is subject to gradual ruination, so the materials selected and the ways in which they come together are a critical part of the design process. An optimal selection of robust architectural materials and enduring installation methods, plus the use of technologies, fault-tolerant systems, and security design to ensure a truly strong structure are crucial for architectural longevity. Without this, buildings simply wouldn't stand the test of time.

Another significant aspect for the lifespan of buildings is their cultural environments. Durability is just as much about cultural attachment as it is the technical ability to endure. Good architecture generates connections between the built environment and its users: strategic approaches to design aim to nurture this relationship by welcoming human use and inspiring care. This will undoubtedly result in a user that is more prone to fix, enhance, and develop modifications, and take care of the construction to prolong its life rather than just deciding to tear it down.

However, designing a building that will materially last for generations and that its users feel connected to is simply not enough. In the face of constant economic, cultural, physical, and environmental change, it becomes increasingly important that architecture produces built environments with long life cycles that also embrace the shifts that will inevitably occur over its long lifetime, constantly adapting to ever-shifting needs. In response to the inherent uncertainty of the future, good architecture is designed as a set of components that meets altering needs, one that is sensitive to natural, functional, and aesthetical changes, too. The nature of this condition requires a similar approach: long-lasting buildings that become flexible and dynamic, avoiding programmatic determinism.

Durable architecture should be conceived to last, but not in a state of eternal permanence. Instead, it should evolve, proving itself worthy of lasting long enough to be transformed and taking into account a variety of possible, unpredictable future conditions. The range of possibilities is endless: from adaptability, where new life is given through thoughtful changes in function and reinvention, to evolutive capacity and clever incremental living spaces, durable architecture means designing with the future in mind. The following pages offer a glimpse of what that might look like, showing how contemporary design, materials, construction, and community engagement can help buildings endure and serve their users for longer.

A NEW GALLERY TO PAY HOMAGE TO THE OLD

JAMES-SIMON-GALERIE
DAVID CHIPPERFIELD ARCHITECTS
BERLIN, GERMANY

The James-Simon-Galerie reinterprets the architectural motifs of Berlin's Museum Island to create a harmonious contemporary entrance for the UNESCO World Heritage Site. The site's original program was built between 1823 and 1930 as a precinct for the arts and sciences and has seen the incorporation of designs by eminent architects over the years. In 1999, an ongoing initiative began to repair damage incurred during the Second World War and bring modern functionality to the destination.

Named after one of the city's most important museum benefactors, the James-Simon-Galerie was designed by David Chipperfield Architects and opened in 2019. It functions as both a gallery and entrance site: four of the island's five museums can be reached via its below-ground Archaeological Promenade, situated along the Kupfergraben canal embankment.

The new gallery marks yet another period in the evolution of museum design. Its architectural language "adopts existing elements of Museum Island, making reference to Schinkel, Stüler, and the other architects involved in the island's creation," explain the architects. One of multiple, seamless interventions is its collonaded walkway that adjoins Friedrich August Stüler's Neues Museum design in an elegant meeting of old and new. Together, they form an open courtyard, while on the embankment side, the new colonnades lead into a principal *piano nobile* level. The exterior's homage extends to matching the materials used. "The materiality of the building in reconstituted stone, with natural stone aggregate, blends in with the rich material palette of Museum Island, with its limestone, sandstone, and rendered facades, while smooth in-situ concrete dominates the interior spaces," explain the architects. Over time, the facade will patinate like its sibling buildings on the island, showing markers of its own history.

JAMES SIMON GALERIE
GEÖFFNET OPEN
Neuer Eingang
New Entrance
PERGAMON MUSEUM
JAMES-SIMON-GALERIE

JAMES-SIMON-GALERIE

The James-Simon-Galerie provides Berlin's historic Museum Island with an official entrance (previous page) and an underground passage to link the cultural complex (opposite, top). Built, like its predecessors, using local limestone and sandstone, the new structure sits flush with the historic Pergamon Museum along the Kupfergraben canal, where a collonaded walkway forms a *piano nobile* (above and opposite, bottom) in a contemporary extension of the old.

A WEATHERPROOF WIND-DOWN RETREAT

THE WANDERING WALLS BED AND BREAKFAST

XRANGE

HENGCHUN, TAIWAN

Looking out from a gusty oceanfront mountaintop, Wandering Walls Bed and Breakfast offers a calm refuge from its dramatic outdoor setting. Located in Hengchun in southern Taiwan, it faces the South China Sea and sits on a previously undeveloped site in-between tall grasses and acacia forests. Set within this rugged context, the curvaceous, eight-room retreat is the design of Taipei-based studio XRANGE Architects and strives to "blur the boundaries between architecture and landscape to define public and private spaces," the architects say.

The stark, solid form aims to match the building's raw environs, creating what its creators term "a sense of quietude and permanence with a single architectural element [the curved walls that are its structure and form] and a minimal palette of materials [concrete, metal, wood, tiles]." The building is cleverly sealed to the elements on the windward side, and instead the outdoors is integrated via stairwell viewpoints, floor-to-ceiling glazing, and tranquil ground-floor patios.

The building's form and materials were determined by the site's challenging climate and limited resources. "The remote location is susceptible to gale-force winter winds, sea salt in the atmosphere, and had no access road prior to construction," explain the architects. "Furthermore, the lack of skilled construction labor and the shoestring-project budget drove the decision to use cast-in-place concrete for its climatic endurance, and ease of transport, and storage." What might have been restrictive conditions have instead furnished the building with its unique character. "The highly tolerant formwork system allows for misalignments and mistakes made by the local workers, which created the signature 'lo-res' curves throughout." The harsh winds, meanwhile, provide their own kind of finishing. "The roughened cast textures of the walls have gradually smoothened out due to their constant stripping by the seasonal winds."

THE WANDERING WALLS
BED AND BREAKFAST

The Wandering Walls Bed and Breakfast sits on the blustery cliffside grasslands (previous page), overlooking the South China Sea (opposite, above) in southern Taiwan. Designed to have minimal impact on its surrounding environment, it is both shaded and protected by the coastal acacia forest (above). To shield against the dramatic weather, the building is closed on the windward-facing side, and open on the calmer grassland-facing one (opposite, below).

The rooftop swimming pools and terrace provide breathtaking panoramic views of the land meeting the sea (above).

Contemplative courtyards enliven the protectively sealed, windward-facing side of the bed and breakfast (opposite, bottom left).

As rough in texture as the outside environment, the building's structural elements are made out of cast-in-place concrete (opposite, bottom right).

A MODERN RESIDENCE TO REFLECT THE FUTURE

HAUS 6

SAUERBRUCH HUTTON

BERLIN, GERMANY

Haus 6 is a four-story residence and studio that slots neatly in-between the historic and modern buildings at Werkhof L57, a creative locale in Berlin. The site's former 19th-century Prussian barracks were left derelict after the Second World War and were revived by the artistic community of West Berlin. In the new millennium, the local, creative neighborhood took this further, rejuvenating the area by purchasing the land and constructing creatively utilitarian buildings for work and housing. Haus 6 was the third project in the Werkhof to be designed by Sauerbruch Hutton, whose studio is housed in the historic red-brick building adjacent.

Due to the period character of the site, the design of Haus 6 was required to conform to the existing profiles of the surrounding buildings, including the red-brick structure and a modern concrete building. "Its height and roof shape mediate between these two neighbors, while its strictly rectangular volume respects the regular forms of the former military compound," Sauerbruch Hutton explains. The result is a simple, durable form, inspired by the original barracks buildings themselves, but with a finish that renders it timeless—however its environment may change. "Its subtly wavy cladding of stainless steel sheet reflects the surroundings irregularly and thereby lends the facade a fluid character."

Inside the 14 units, occupied by individuals and families across the creative industries from architecture to music and sociology, required similarly versatile designs. "The units display a variety of interior layouts, reflecting the range of different ideas that individual members of the group had about the way in which they want to live and work," the architects say. "What they all had in common was a desire for maximum flexibility and freedom in the division and use of the spaces, also in the long term."

To create a building that was both adaptable yet lasting, the architects used prestressed concrete slabs that left the spacious, 47 × 10 m (154 × 33 ft) floor area free of structural columns. To maximize the space, service shafts were installed within the depth of the facade. Each of the eight flats permitted per floor are afforded outlooks to the north and south by another clever quirk: the apartments are accessed not by internal corridors, but via balconies on the south facade that link up to a central staircase. These outdoor spaces are flexible, and can either be used as private or communal zones by the occupants.

Haus 6 in Berlin provides its residents with flexible indoor-outdoor spaces for living and work (above and opposite). Vaulted gallery-like interior spaces cater to the inhabitants who work across the creative industries (page 51, top, and opposite page, bottom). Encased in reflective covering, the building's facade blends into the historic site, acting as a playful mirror (page 50 and opposite, bottom left).

A HOSPITAL DESIGN THAT CARES FOR THE CITY

FUNDACIÓN SANTA FE DE BOGOTÁ
EL EQUIPO DE MAZZANTI
BOGOTÁ, COLOMBIA

The expansion of the Fundación Santa Fe de Bogotá (Santa Fe de Bogotá Foundation) hospital connects an old structure to a new build, private care to public utility, and patients to better recovery. The 12-story building was conceived as part of an architectural competition launched by the foundation in 2012, seeking an innovative brick extension for the hospital that could flow from the existing structure and improve patient care. Designing the expansion proved challenging, say architects El Equipo de Mazzanti, "because more than being a building, it had to connect at an urban level, to merge with the existing hospital, and to project itself for future space requirements."

The new brick facade is a seamless, yet newly characterful, extension of the old. Supported by metallic parts and cables, brickwork is used as a veil over the glass and concrete structure that enables controlled light to filter through. "This allows us to have different patterns and textures giving the opportunity to have several natural lighting uses." The new building houses neonatal, child, and adult ICUs, as well as cardiology, gynecology, and psychiatry, and an auditorium and medical lounge. On the ninth floor, a solarium "tries to recover the garden hospital concept, reducing patients' stress and confinement conditions," explain the architects. The building prioritizes light conditions, spatiality, and nature based on positive statistical research into the reduction of recovery time, infections, and medical complications.

The extension is located in dense, central Bogota, between the Ninth and Seventh Avenue, and services the public and pedestrian flow with a ground-level plaza. The space is an "urban connector," comprising a large urban corridor, generous green spaces, commercial services, a coffee shop, and an auditorium. In this manner, lasting care is extended beyond patients, with a public-serving design that embeds the hospital in its urban setting.

FUNDACIÓN
SANTA FE DE BOGOTÁ

The new, mixed-use wing of the Fundación Santa Fe de Bogotá hospital improves patient care on the inside, while providing for the general public on the outside, with a connective urban corridor and plaza (previous page). The structure is veiled in brick netting that allows restorative natural light to filter in (below), while a multi-level indoor garden, accessible to the convalescing and their families, furthers the plan for holistic care (opposite page, bottom).

Welcome
Bienvenido

IN CUBA, AN ARCHITECTURAL BEACON OF HOPE

CASA TORRE
ALBOR ARQUITECTOS
CIENFUEGOS, CUBA

Casa Torre (Tower House) in Cienfuegos uses vertical-planning to provide a family with a house that can adapt to the challenges of Cuban life. Designed by local studio Albor Arquitectos, the tower is a symbol of hope and offers a meditation on, and response to, its environment. "At Albor, we believe it is within this hostile context that the architecture that interests us can be produced. Architecture based on proximity to people and the prevailing social reality, the continuity of the inherited city, the rediscovery of construction techniques of the past through worker-architect feedback, the resolution of problems with a certain dignity—the aspiration for a kind of noble beauty emanating from reality," they explain.

The tower structure was chosen to maximize space for the family on the small, allocated plot, and opens up to 88 m² (947 ft²) of living space. The house is made of cool, exposed concrete, and is built on a narrow city block that previously housed a prefabricated structure and backyard. Elegant louvered shutters cut through the facade, referencing Cuba's iconic architecture and providing ventilation and shaded light. The ground floor houses the main living space, made up of the kitchen and dining area, extending onto a green, shaded terrace. The plants from the terrace grow up the building, forming a lush vertical garden.

The two upstairs levels are adaptable and were "conceived to accommodate various situations of family coexistence." They may be arranged into different permutations, including two bedrooms in one room, a workspace plus a bedroom, or additional bedrooms to be rented out for extra income. On top is a roof terrace with views across the city to the sea. "The volume of the house, turned into a tower, is the resulting expression of the desire for a house with a garden overlooking the landscape in a very compact urban nucleus, in an almost naive gesture of establishing contact with a timeless reality," explain the architects.

CASA TORRE

Casa Torre is a multi-level family home that overlooks the Cuban town of Cienfuegos (opposite) and offers panoramic rooftop views to the sea (previous page and opposite, bottom right). The interior spaces are designed with mixed-uses and adaptability in mind, while the adjacent courtyard garden (opposite page, top) casts its greenery up the building to form a joyful vertical garden (opposite, bottom left).

THE SUPERADOBE DOMES OF HORMUZ

PRESENCE IN HORMUZ
ZAV ARCHITECTS
HORMUZ, IRAN

Presence is a tourism complex built on the island of Hormuz, Iran, to stimulate the local economy and offer more autonomy to the community. The island is located on its namesake strait, which is the key passage for Middle Eastern petroleum exportation. It is a site of geological wonder, made up of colorful landscapes including an ochre-red beach and rainbow mountains. After centuries of use as a strategic docking point, the island fell into decline when the nearby mainland city, Bandar Abbas, was developed into a key port. Today, the island is both a tourist destination and politically strategic location. However, its limited job opportunities mean that locals have frequently turned to illegal seafaring activities for income.

As such, a semi-public institution commissioned ZAV Architects to create an urban-development design that would empower the island's residents. Included is a culturally rich accommodation complex, called the Majara Residence, to attract tourists, allow long-term revenue, and importantly, engage the local community as its custodians. "Presence in Hormuz is a continuous process aimed at building trust rather than architectural objects, in order to encourage the participation of local people," explain the architects.

The complex is made up of multicolored dome-shaped dwellings that honor regional architectural forms and the island's chromatic geography. The structures were created using the "superadobe" technique pioneered by Iranian architect Nader Khalili, in which earth-filled sandbags are coiled and layered with barbed wire that acts as both support and mortar, providing double the strength of a pitched-roof house. The sandbags were filled with earth dredged from Hormuz's own port, which provides thermal insulation and is both fire and flood-proof. The low-cost building method prioritized budget for training and labor, empowering and involving local craftspeople who are now experts in the building technique.

PRESENCE IN HORMUZ

Presence in Hormuz is a tourism complex built to enliven the Iranian island's economy. The chromatic ensemble of domed accommodation structures references the island's unique, wondrous geology (previous page and opposite, top) and local architecture.

The complex was built by newly trained locals, using the thermally efficient, flood- and fire-proof superadobe technique pioneered in Iran.

GOOD ARCHITECTURE IS HOLISTIC

Holistic architecture strikes the perfect balance between form and function. It exists in harmony with its setting, inside and out

Today, the majority of the world's population lives in cities, replete with pollution, over-population, and increasingly fast-paced lives. As such, achieving a healthy lifestyle has become one of the urban dweller's most preoccupying goals—which is where the notion of holistic living comes in. Taking a holistic view means looking at the "whole picture," understanding that each of the parts that make a whole are connected and interdependent (i.e. that the whole is also only recognizable as a sum of its parts). Science, medicine, nature, technology, and countless other facets of our existence are all fields made up of thousands of intricate parts that exist so that they can function and evolve properly.

Nowhere is this more apparent than in the realms of architecture and design. Design is everywhere, from the objects that we use to the spaces that we inhabit. And architecture, with its potential to protect, inspire, and shape behavior, can—and should—play a vital role in ensuring the overall wellbeing of its users. Moreover, a building, no matter its intended function, should always be conceptualized as a whole, meaning that all structures, materials, elements, uses, and concepts are carefully considered in relation to one and other, and must serve a meaningful purpose.

Le Corbusier's concept of *machine-à-habiter* made reference to the way a modern building should be. Houses, he posited, should be viewed as machines for living, and as with machines, each and every part should be considered of equal importance to ensure the smooth functioning of the whole. This idea brought along the notion of useful and good design, whereby all necessary parts function exactly as they should, and all unnecessary elements are abandoned.

Since this concept was first introduced, the world has evolved rapidly, and it would therefore be superficial not to go beyond it. The complexity of current ways of living demand the contemplation of the psychology of design, the importance of human interaction, and the way users relate to their space and its surroundings. In order to create a harmonious coexistence between all its elements, good architecture has to be holistic—not only for its inhabitants but also in order for it to be coherent within its time and context. The combination of all these elements is what constitutes outstanding building design.

A successful architectural project serves a specific need: it has a particular program, and a list of requirements to achieve. The building's distinct form must respond to this in a way that allows all of these criteria to be met. Additionally, the materials and the construction techniques used are what make a project tangible. As such, all of these elements must be carefully chosen so that there's an equilibrium between the built project and its use, and so that each part enhances and contributes to the project's purpose.

When considering the nature of holistic architecture, it is vital to consider how a building is supposed to function. Good architectural solutions respect their surroundings, be they urban, suburban, or rural. Whether employing local materials or labor, best-practice projects respond to their environment while blending into it. The relationship between the building and its context is reflected in how its community interacts with its exterior. By effectively connecting interior and outside spaces (e.g. by providing proper ventilation, integrating natural elements, and creating useful programs for the "in-between" spaces), designers can create healthy environments for their building's users.

Moreover, interiors should be designed for comfort in every possible way, from an aesthetically pleasing conception to the accurate incorporation of light, acoustic, and thermal conditioning. Elements such as furniture and useful objects should be optimized to fulfill users' needs while maintaining harmony with the space they are in.

The meticulous consideration of all parts, elements, and concepts is what makes good architecture holistic. To achieve this, architects must pursue precise decisions that have an impactful meaning on the building's overall design, as well as embracing human wellbeing and site preservation as top priorities. Ultimately, as the following projects demonstrate, it is about considering architecture as a series of processes, one that is aligned with contexts, users, eras, functions, and—consequently—with the idiosyncratic significance of the individual building in question itself.

A HARMONIOUS RAINFOREST RETREAT

JUNGLE HOUSE

STUDIO MK27 – MARCIO KOGAN + SAMANTA CAFARDO

GUARUJÁ, BRAZIL

Jungle House slots gently into the rainforest canopy with a thoughtful design. The sprawling home in Guarujá, on the southeastern coast of Brazil, was designed by Studio MK27. "The introduction of this house to this landscape has the objective of optimizing the connection between architecture and nature, privileging the view looking out to the ocean and the incidence of sunlight in the internal spaces," explain the architects.

Constructed using concrete and wood, the building repurposed a previously cleared site. "The main volume of the house is elevated from the ground and seems built into the topography. The house, therefore, projects itself out from the mountain," explain the architects. The decking, for example, was shaped to "respect the existing land" and foster an organic interaction between nature and the man-made elements. A mere two supporting pillars bear the weight of the part jutting from the mountain.

The three-story layout repeats the external materiality, keeping cool with concrete and adding warmth with wood. In dialogue with the exterior, its various features adapt to the tropical climate. The ground floor houses a covered wooden terrace, a children's play room, and utilities. The first floor contains a large TV room and six bedrooms; five of these flow into a veranda, where a hammock sways in front of shaded blinds, mounted as folding doors. But it is the third floor, nestled underneath the green roof, that exemplifies the nature-bound building's ethos. The social area of the house opens up on both sides to the contrasting natural elements via a generous wooden deck, offering a swimming pool, hot tub, living room, and kitchen. "This last floor offers a spatial sensation which synthesizes the principles of the house. This social space has a radical relation with nature, by means of both the view of the ocean as well as the proximity to the forest in the mountain," says Studio MK27.

JUNGLE HOUSE

Jungle House is a Brazilian home that enhances the interaction between architecture and nature, connecting its residents to the rainforested mountainside via walkways, slatted-wooden balconies, and expansive, stacked rooftop terraces (previous page). Inside the open-plan living space, floor-to-ceiling, dual aspect glazing provides views to the trees and out towards the ocean (above).

A GALLERY CAST BY DESERT SANDS

35 GREEN CORNER BUILDING

STUDIO ANNE HOLTROP

MUHARRAQ, BAHRAIN

Cast from sand, 35 Green Corner Building is a site-specific structure that stands in material communion with the low-lying, desert-swathed environs of Bahrain. The public building, located in Muharraq, Bahrain's third largest city, was designed by Studio Anne Holtrop, and houses part of the art collection from the Shaikh Ebrahim Center for Culture and Research. It is situated close to its namesake, the Green Gate, a vertical garden designed by Patrick Blanc.

The narrow, low-profile building is decidedly sculptural inside and out, sticking to a restrained three-material design that slots seamlessly into its sun-bleached, urban surroundings. The plan consists of one long, main facade, two short-ended facades, and two identically sized interior rooms that are separated by the building's core. To maximize the impact of the compact space, Studio Anne Holtrop sought to make the facade itself the "main spatial element." For the form, it looked to the ground beneath, employing a site-driven technique. To give every wall a unique relief, sand was poured in situ into the edges of the cast concrete slabs. "The elements are cast on the ground next to the building. Each cast results in a unique imprint on the element. At the position of the windows and the corners of the building, the relief is visible, as a geological cut in the ground," Anne Holtrop explains. The result, on the exterior, is a harmonious contrasting of the neat, horizontal slabs that demarcate each of the four floors and rooftop, and the organically chiseled facades, resembling rock faces. Beyond creating a one-of-a-kind, site-specific work, the sand-casting proved efficient, cutting down on transport and energy costs.

The technique was employed broadly throughout the building to create the textural interior's ceilings, walls, and flooring. The result is a building in tune, not only with its environment, but with itself, providing a restrained yet characterful setting for the art to shine. Sand too wrought the building's fixtures: built off-site by the Kemner Foundry, these include its large, movable shutters and luminous, square door—both made of sand-cast aluminum—that marks the entrance to the structure. Where the concrete elements are solid and convex, the aluminum casts are hollow, their interior visible through the windows. Inside, the relief-bearing walls and ceiling are broken up by large square windows that look out over Muharraq, capturing its similarly muted, light-reflecting cityscape.

A sculptural gallery space, 35 Green Corner Building is located in Bahrain. The facade is composed of naturalistic concrete blocks, cast on site in the sandy ground, that are stacked between concrete slabs and punctuated by square windows (page 72). This technique also created the textured reliefs of the interior walls (opposite, top, and previous page, bottom) and the aluminum door (opposite, bottom left).

JEANNE GANG: AN ARCHITECT FOR CHANGE

The American architect and founder of Studio Gang creates spaces with the firm belief that good design can shape societies and communities for the better

Born in 1964, in the Midwest of the United States, architect, MacArthur Fellow, and Studio Gang founder Jeanne Gang describes herself as being on the cusp of generational difference, "I'm between Gen X and Baby Boomer. I feel more Gen X, somehow. I don't know why." Looking at her portfolio of socially progressive, experiential projects, the answer might sit in the values represented in her work reimagining public spaces. While Boomers are typically thought to value career success, competitiveness, and personal gratification, Gen X-ers are more likely to view life from a more holistic perspective, focusing on work-life balance, flexibility, and diversity. Gang is widely known for her firm belief that architecture can, and should, be responsible for positive social change.

In a 2019 article for *New York Magazine*, Justin Davidson describes Gang's work as, "An ongoing negotiation with nature." Looking at the sinuous, organic lines found in projects such as Chicago's Aqua Tower and San Francisco's MIRA, as well as the earthy textures of New York's Richard Gilder Center for Science, Education, and Innovation at the American Museum

Gang's undulating design for the Richard Gilder Center for Science, Education, and Innovation (above) sits at the physical heart of the American Museum of Natural History, New York. As in Gang's other designs—like Chicago's Aqua Tower (previous page and opposite, bottom), which references the striated limestone outcroppings of the Great Lakes area—the Gilder Center's canyon-like form (opposite, top) draws on natural processes such as weathering and erosion.

of Natural History, it's easy to see how the architect's adventurous rural childhood fused with her early exposure to engineering. Gang and her three sisters were raised by their mother—a teacher—and their engineer father. "I was really influenced by my landscape, my setting, my home city, which was Chicago—not that I grew up in the city, but that was my go-to city for architecture and museums. I was also very influenced by being around nature. Because I lived pretty far away from the city, I was an 'outside' kid. I think my father was probably my biggest influence. He was an engineer and I remember always going to his office and playing with the big pieces of paper that they had, and an electric eraser—things like that. I was constantly making structures, like a tree house or snow castles. We also traveled a lot, on road trips, so I saw these big landscapes and all the bridges that my dad wanted to go visit. You name it, we saw the bridge."

Following in her father's footsteps, Gang initially applied, and was accepted, to study engineering at the University of Illinois. A change of heart saw her take on architecture, where she found her calling. "I have a Bachelor of Science in Architecture. During undergrad, I studied abroad for one year in France, in the Versailles program—the University of Illinois had a school there—and that's when I fell head over heels in love with architecture—and Paris," she adds. "When you look at architecture, it tells you something about people, culture, art, engineering—all of those things. It embodies who we are."

Gang went on to become a Rotary Foundation Ambassadorial scholar at the Swiss Federal Institute of Technology in Zürich, Switzerland, before applying to graduate school and receiving her Masters Degree in Architecture from the prestigious Harvard Graduate School of Design in 1993.

Drawn to the unique crucible of ideas, philosophies, experimentation, and innovation that academic environments can often provide, Gang has since returned to the Harvard Graduate School of Design as a Professor in Practice. "I went away for a long time and taught in a lot of different places, teaching every couple of years to continue making academia part of my work in architecture. It's still about ideas and dialogue and thinking. It's not just about producing buildings. It's asking, why are we doing it? Working with colleagues at the GSD, and with students, has been a wonderful way to continue that conversation." Reflecting on how diversity of thought and process has shaped her career, she continues: "My practice has always been about bringing other fields into design, and seeing architecture as part of a whole ecosystem of practices. That's a lot easier in an academic setting. For sure, you can find it elsewhere, but people in academia are always ready for that conversation."

Following her graduation from Harvard, Gang relocated to the Netherlands, where she began working for famed architect Rem Koolhas at OMA. There, she worked on the Lille Grand Palais and Maison à Bordeaux. In 1997, Gang founded her own practice, Studio Gang, with headquarters in Chicago, and now offices in New York, San Francisco, and Paris. In addition to wanting to "not work for men, frankly," it was the architect's desire to create in a whole new way that inspired her to go it alone. "I wanted to do it my way. I was just so driven to do my own work, since very early on. And so I did." In 2018, in an article she wrote for *Fast Company,* Gang announced that they had closed the pay gap at Studio Gang, and called for other practices to do the same.

Gang's projects are fiercely modern, and yet perfectly formed to serve the people that use them. With a heavy focus on context and conversation, the processes undertaken at the studio are held up by two key pillars: extensive research and collaboration. The architect equates their success to this democratic approach to design. "People in different professions team up in different ways. It's about listening to other people's experiences. I've taken

Gang's radically contemporary designs are nevertheless entirely mindful of their context and function. The WMS Boathouse at Clark Park (left) is inspired by the rhythm and movement of rowing, and serves as a key public access point along the Chicago River. The Writers Theater (above and page 82, top), with its partially transparent facade and ivy-covered backdrops, powerfully connects with its park setting in Glencoe, Illinois and, at night, emits a warm, inviting glow, drawing the community in.

that into our urban practice over the last 10 years, and really turned it into also engaging with community members. I never felt threatened by these things; I always saw it as an advantage. I was also trying to make the studio represent diversity with different voices, people from different backgrounds, genders, etc. I think that really gives a fuller response to any project."

Touching on the projects that epitomize her research-driven process and strong belief that architecture can be a tool for social change, Gang mentions the Arcus Center for Social Justice Leadership at Kalamazoo College in Michigan, and the Gilder Center for Science, Education, and Innovation, which is currently under construction in New York. "It's a new wing for the complex, 26-building campus of the American Museum of Natural History. This project is all about clarifying how people will move through the space, creating new connections between buildings, and reorganizing the flow of people, so that they can better absorb the entire museum. It's also about responding to what we found when starting the project—that there's a crisis going on in American science education. It's an urgent problem, because it's why people are denying climate change, and why people didn't get vaccinated."

Architecture is an industry steeped in history, much of which has carried forward the weight of tradition. In its most archaic form, a career in architecture has been a career for middle-class white men, where the voices of those in power do not sound like those of the masses, but have dictated how the masses should live. Gang has sought to question our relationship with architecture, challenging not only the status-quo of hierarchical practices, but also the ways we socialize within, learn from, and sustain our built and natural environments.

"When you look at architecture, it tells you something about people, culture, art, engineering—all of those things. It embodies who we are."

Studio Gang takes a research-led approach to design. The gem-like form of Gang's New York office block, Solar Carve (opposite, bottom), was developed through the studio's ongoing tall-building research. Sculpted by the sun's rays, it privileges fresh air and natural light, which it reflects back to its surroundings.

The result of extensive study, the Nature Boardwalk at Lincoln Park Zoo (above) transformed an unsustainable Victorian pond into ecological haven for biodiversity to thrive.

AN AMBITIOUS HIGH-RISE INSPIRED BY A LEAF

ONE HUNDRED
STUDIO GANG
ST. LOUIS, MISSOURI, USA

Taking inspiration from the intricate form of a leaf, One Hundred makes clever use of space to create light-filled and energy-efficient residences that provide every comfort. Located in St. Louis, Missouri, USA, the high-rise building overlooks Forest Park to the west and the Gateway Arch monument to the east. The approximately 115 m (380 ft) building houses 316 residential units, amenities, parking, and retail spaces on ground level that cater to residents and park-goers alike. It is the first work by the Chicago-led Studio Gang, founded by architect Jeanne Gang, in St. Louis. One Hundred is one in a series of buildings that embodies what the studio calls "solar carving," whereby a design is shaped by a site's solar access.

The building's volume is made up of stacked four-story tiers, with glazing that juts outwards on each level articulated like a jagged leaf edge. "The facade is angled to create generous outdoor spaces on top of each tier, providing terraces for a quarter of the apartments, as well as shared amenity space for the resident community atop the green roof podium," explain the architects. "Working to enhance the opportunities provided by the site orientation and environmental forces, the building's leaf-shaped plan and tiered massing maximize its performance, reducing overall energy load and increasing occupant comfort," they add.

The clever use of space allows One Hundred to house generous amenities that cater to a range of lifestyles. On site are recreational spaces such as party rooms, gaming rooms, dining facilities, and outdoor decks, as well as health utilities such as a fitness room and personal training facility, a pool, and professional amenities including a business lounge and conference room. In a rare, democratic act, each apartment contains a corner living room with floor-to-ceiling glazing that brings in panoramic views of Forest Park and Gateway Arch. The double exposures provide the added benefit of allowing natural light to flood in daily.

The tower, though dramatic in its fanned, angular form, finds gentle interaction with its environment. The glazing is intended to provide pleasing reflections of the changing scenery, creating a tessellated array of patterns and colors as the parks' foliage morphs throughout the year. The public and retail spaces on the ground level expand the footprint of the building to the civic space, offering a gateway from the Central West End neighborhood to the parklands.

THE COWORKING SPACE, TURNED INSIDE OUT

SECOND HOME HOLLYWOOD

SELGASCANO

LOS ANGELES, CALIFORNIA, USA

Second Home Hollywood is a coworking space dedicated to providing a healthier place of work by positioning nature at the office-worker's doorstep. The East Hollywood building radically prioritizes the outdoors over the interior to create a sustainable, nature-bound workplace to boost wellbeing, while simultaneously providing a blueprint for the revitalization of concrete urban areas. "The interior spaces in this project go pretty much unnoticed and the main focus is outdoors, which is quintessential to the living style in Los Angeles," explain Selgascano architects.

The 8,436 m² (90,800 ft²) site includes a 1964 building by Paul R. Williams, the first recognized African-American architect working in Los Angeles, which has been preserved as the core of the campus, forming its entrance. The existing building houses 320 "roaming places" on the ground floor, with an additional 200 workspaces on the first floor. Common facilities, including a cafe, bar, restaurant, event and conference hall, as well as rest and leisure areas, and open terraces are located all around the complex. The second building, erected above an existing parking lot, was demolished to make way for 60 oval-shaped, transparent-walled office and meeting room pods that provide space for up to 700 people to work. The pods are dotted throughout a lush garden, built on top of 1.2 m (4 ft) of soil compacted onto the car park, and have glass walls that provide panoramic views of the greenery outdoors. The clear facades reduce the need for artificial lighting and include operable openings for cross-ventilation.

"In Second Home Hollywood, instead of bringing the garden inside the office, we have brought the office out to the garden," explain the architects. The green space provides a vital lung to its East Hollywood setting, replacing "90,800 ft² [8,436 m²] of hardscape for 70,000 ft² [6,503 m²] of landscape." Meanwhile, the site can collect and store 140,060 l (30,809 gal) of water in cisterns that can be used for irrigation. The flourishing garden is a biodiverse one, home to 10,000 plants and trees, as well as butterflies, ants, bees, and squirrels.

The campus dramatically breaks up the surrounding concrete jungle, enlivening the area with its yellow roofs and heaving plant life. "What previously was a parking lot is now a garden. It is one of the few private developments in history in which the footprint of the built-environment has been returned to the natural environment," say the architects.

KDOC

SECOND HOME HOLLYWOOD

The Second Home Hollywood co-working space envelopes office work with nature. In addition to preserving an existing, period piece of architecture, the program includes 60 transparent, cheerfully yellow-roofed pods. Situated within a biodiverse garden that covers an underground parking lot (opposite), it acts as a vital green lung for the surrounding urban context and adjacent highway (previous page).

AN ODE TO NATURE, THE GREAT COMPOSER

CHAPEL OF SOUND
OPEN ARCHITECTURE
CHENGDE, CHINA

Set in a valley, the monolithic Chapel of Sound provides an acoustic experience following nature's score. Built by Beijing-based OPEN Architecture, the concert hall near Chengde, China, was designed to enhance active and passive auditory experiences, hosting musical performances and amplifying nature's own concertos. "We did not want the definition of the space to be absolute. Solitary or communal, music or the sound of nature, gazing into the starry sky or connecting with one's inner self—it's open to the interpretation of the users," explain OPEN's founding partners Li Hu and Huang Wenjing.

It was the architects' wish that the man-made structure appear like a boulder that had simply rolled into place on site. The building is made from concrete enhanced with local mineral-rich rock, and composed of a harmonious inner and outer shell. The jagged, striated exterior references the surrounding mountains and creates structural, cantilevered support by expanding out into an expertly engineered inverted cone, conceived alongside designers Arup.

The physics of sound in nature provided the final inspiration for the building's shape. Li and Huang found spatial guidance in the natural reverberation of caves. They worked with sound engineers to create defined openings in the building that absorb sound. This allowed them to forgo the acoustic materials traditionally used in concert halls, rendering the cavernous stone interior tranquil and harmonious.

The openings also bring light into the concert hall, while framing the magnificent landscape beyond. The building is sustainably simple too. It requires no heating or cooling and uses a Pantheon-inspired drainage system to dispel any rainwater that enters through its upper void. Other key features include a semi-outdoor amphitheater, an outdoor stage, a green room, and viewing platforms. Winding staircases weave through the space, warmed with bronze finishes, and lead up to the roof platform with its panoramic views of the valley and the Great Wall.

CHAPEL OF SOUND

The Chapel of Sound is a naturalistic concert hall set deep in a valley (previous page) near Chengde, China. Its striated exterior (opposite, bottom) references the geology of its striking mountainscape setting (opposite page, top). Inside, the semi-outdoor amphitheater (above) provides advanced acoustics by taking structural inspiration from the reverberation of sound in caves.

THE INDOOR-OUTDOOR HOME

CASA UC

DANIELA BUCIO SISTOS

MORELIA, MEXICO

Casa UC is a fluid indoor-outdoor floor plan that engages the senses. It lies on the outskirts of Morelia in Michoacán, Mexico, and was designed by Daniela Bucio Sistos, who received a commission for a tranquil, single-level family home that could house a vast collection of books.

The result is a secluded house begging to be explored. "Casa UC doesn't say much on the outside. The main entrance is tucked in at the end of the textured partition wall that runs along most of the front of the property," explains the architect's studio. The inside, accessed via a ramp, leads down to the heart of the home: a central courtyard where a royal poinciana grows beneath an elevated circular roof. "From the vestibule two large circular openings can be seen on the sides, one inside the library and one at the end of the patio that connects to the secondary bedrooms," says the studio. "The circular foyer is the guiding axis of the residence, and symbolically it is taken as the starting point for the radial floor that runs throughout the project." In the outdoor courtyard, covered passageways blur inside and out, connecting to the bedrooms, kitchen, and living area, and the outdoor terrace leading down to a sloping cypress-tree garden below.

The layout creates what the architect refers to as "micro-environments," all drifting outwards from the courtyard. In each of these, Sistos sought to create "contemplative and silent" spaces that would engage multiple senses. To do so, she applied texture, scale, a richly earthy palette, the presence of the "outdoors-in," and, of course, a roaming layout. The house remains cohesive through its restrained—but inviting—palette, one driven by the natural colors of local materials such as stone, brick, and copper. Sistos "sought to create an almost mono-chromatic residence, but full of textures so that with the incidence of natural light on the different volumes, the project would have different personalities through-out the day," the studio suggests.

Casa UC is a single-level family home in Michoacán, Mexico, that fluidly fuses the indoors and outdoors. Warm brick passages with slatted-wooden roofs (opposite) lead from its private quarters to the heart of the home: a circular courtyard where a single royal poinsettia grows (above). At the rear of the house, the open-plan living area and outdoor terrace overlook a sloping cypress garden.

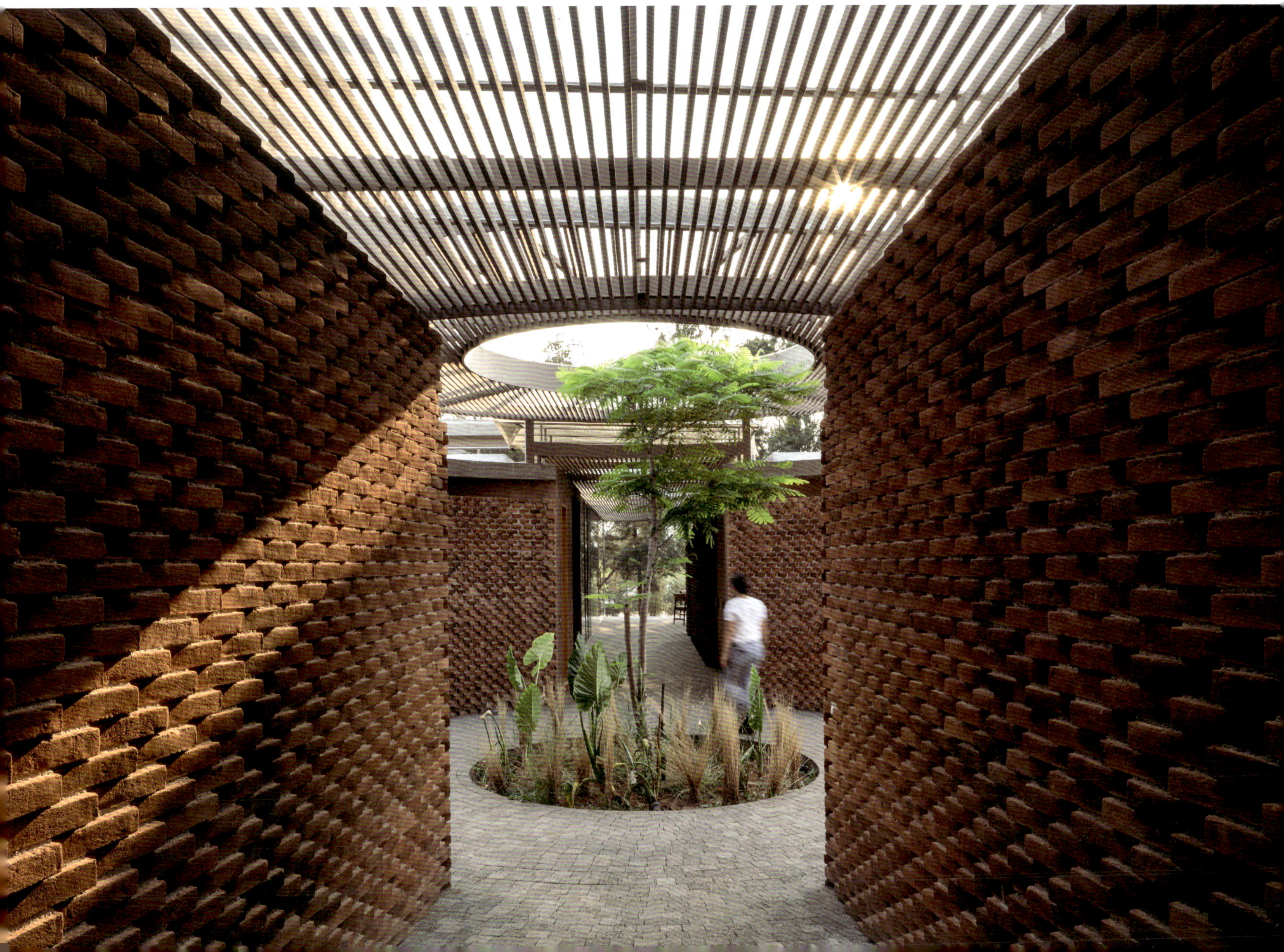

GEOMETRY UNDER THE ALENTEJO SUN

HOUSE IN GRÂNDOLA
BAK GORDON ARQUITECTOS
GRÂNDOLA, PORTUGAL

Built of local materials, the House in Grândola is a coherent and geometric family home built to endure—and celebrate—its environment. The 375 m² (4,036 ft²) building is located in Monte dos Patos, Grândola, in Portugal's huge southern region of Alentejo. A hot, rural area on the Atlantic coastline, Alentejo's land is quarried for limestone, marble, and copper, while one of its greatest exports is cork, its trees producing two thirds of the world's entire cork supply.

To create a building that could withstand the parched, sun-baked conditions, Lisbon-based studio Bak Gordon Arquitectos took cues from such endemic materials. The resulting house is clad in lime mortar and insulated with cork from the outside. Depending on the light, it takes on the dusty hues of the land, ranging from a pale, sun-bleached peach to a deep, rusty rose. The striking geometry of the T-shaped house is at once clear from the long, diamond-shaped pool that faces south, where blue water meets dusty earth just as Alentejo reaches the Atlantic. Against the "vast territory of Alentejo, the house emerges from an extensive pool leaning against a wall facing south, as if it were a sounding board for the entire landscape," the architects explain of their poetic vision.

The structure of the house juts out of this swimming pool and is reached by two indoor/outdoor rooms, akin to vestibules, on either wing of the house. According to the architects, the spaces "act as places as transition between interior and exterior," rendering them ideal spots for rest and relaxation. These liminal rooms are shaded by wooden pergolas that cast changing shadows throughout the day. The weatherproofing is vital for summertime in the region, when temperatures regularly exceed 40°C (104°F). The walls of the leisurely structures are thronged by inbuilt seating for relaxation, while large square cutouts bring in light and allow views to the countryside.

The interior areas of the house are laid around a small courtyard, with a petite, corner pond. The geometric building was arranged at different heights to accomodate for the sloping land beneath it, but inside feels wholly unified. The materiality of the building brings the tones of the outside in, while the layout serves to counteract the harsh elements. Two shaded recesses on the east and west axes allow daylight to gently enter the building and bounce into the patio, directed by curved walls—a clever route that leaves the building well-lit but cool.

House in Grândola is a geometric family home built to withstand the harsh conditions of sun-soaked coastal Alentejo in southern Portugal. The shielding house blends into the surrounding landscape, clad in local lime mortar and insulating cork (opposite, top). A long, cooling swimming pool lines the southern-edge of the house (previous page and opposite, bottom), accessible from one of two shaded indoor-outdoor rooms (above) on either wing of the T-shaped structure.

GOOD ARCHITECTURE IS INCLUSIVE

Inclusive architecture requires careful thought and acute sensitivity. It understands and supports the many different ways of living and operating in today's world

The perameters of architecture are constantly shifting, catering to the needs and desires of the different eras and societies for whom its buildings are created. Regardless of time or place, however, architecture has often proved an exclusive practice. Yet, as a consequence of the information revolution, the widespread exclusion of minority communities has become more evident than ever before, sparking debates on what a more inclusive world should look like, and how architecture can help facilitate it.

Although inclusion is a concept too complex to be enacted through building alone, the physical spaces we occupy are fundamental in establishing the behaviors and habits we come to consider the "norm." For instance, once upon a time, homes would be equipped with both a dining room and kitchen, whereas today, as a result of changing attitudes to communal eating, as well as a lack of space, many simply only have kitchens, which serve as both. As such, architects have considerable power when it comes to altering societal perceptions. In recent years we have experienced a paradigm shift not only in the design but also in the production of spaces, which has led us to question whether modern cities, and their architecture, are truly inclusive. The global phenomenon in major cities of spiraling rents, lack of social housing, and the unaffordability of mortgages, has started to push people out of urban centers. In 2021, a report by accountancy firm PricewaterhouseCoopers estimated that, impacted by the pandemic and work-from-home freedom, up to 300,000 Londoners could flee the capital, a claim echoed in another report by the London Assembly that year, suggesting 15 percent of residents wanted to leave.

To pave the way toward an architecture for all, it is essential to recognize that everyone deserves the right to enjoy the same access to spaces that shelter, satisfy, and stimulate regardless of their class, their physique, their social status, their culture, their race, their sexuality, and/or their gender identity. Although in many cities there is already a legal framework in place that ensures at least basic accessibility rights for people with disabilities, it is clear that there is still a long way to go, both socially and culturally, when it comes to constructing spaces that really are designed for everyone.

When talking about inclusive architecture, it is important not simply to take into account the laws and cultural etiquette of different countries and peoples, but also to expand our gaze to incorporate the many diverse ways of living and operating within the world at large. The creation of more accessible built environments requires an empathetic and sensitive approach at every stage of the design process, from the choice of materials to the layout. Good architecture should never isolate, but must engage and communicate.

As demonstrated in this section, truly inclusive buildings range from those that are welcoming and communicative in both form and function, to those that create space, connection, and opportunity. They might facilitate better education, or offer users the chance to enjoy culture in remote areas where previously such opportunities didn't exist. They might take the form of attractive public leisure spaces in big cities, or uphold the values and requirements of minority communities, allowing them not only to enjoy better modes of living but to thrive. They proffer new ways of bringing people (and sometimes other life forms) together, promoting equity and peaceful coexistence.

Although it is true that there are political, social, and economic issues that architecture cannot single-handedly ameliorate, it is important to recognize that, with careful thought, creating built environments that recognize the many different ways of inhabiting the world is both feasible and affordable. Inclusive architecture requires that spaces are designed according to a set of accessibility criteria that meet the needs of a diverse user; it does not prioritize one sector of society in particular, but instead finds a way to encompass them all. It must nurture and protect people of every kind of identity and income bracket. It should quash rather than further discrimination, inviting and uplifting the many, not the few.

A CAR PARK BECOMES AN URBAN PLAYGROUND

ISRAELS PLADS
COBE + SWECO ARCHITECTS
COPENHAGEN, DENMARK

Central Copenhagen has transformed a carpark into a multi-purpose civic leisure space. The plaza bridges the bustling locations of Ørstedsparken (a park), Copenhagen University, various schools, and the Torvehallerne market, and is a response to increasing urban density in the Danish capital. "Copenhagen has a goal for its residents to spend 20 percent more time in public spaces by 2025," says COBE, who created the design along with Sweco Architects. "The obvious solution to the densification is smarter ways of sharing spaces—over the days, weeks, months, and years."

Today, the carpark still services the public, but it has been relocated underground, and can be accessed from the street by a spiral ramp. Instead, the granite plaza has been built hovering over the top, above the existing street level, with connecting border inclines to the street. Its relation to the green space of Ørstedsparken is equally thoughtful. "The plaza also works as a transition between two worlds, the city, and the neighboring park," explains COBE. "The landscape character of the park continues into the plaza in the form of the organic pattern of trees."

The space purposefully encourages wide public use. In the center of the plaza is the large urban playground made up of basketball and football courts, a ball cage, children's playground, and skating area. "Unique facilities have been created to inspire and encourage movement and exercise—formal or informal." The park also offers multiple spaces for relaxation, from social seating areas beneath the trees and along the square's outskirts, to large open spaces for gatherings and markets. As intended, it is a smarter way of sharing space that has been successfully taken up by its public. "Israels Plads [serves] as a schoolyard during the daytime, a public basketball court in the afternoon, and a dining room in the evening, a skate park during the weekday, and a flea market during the weekend," says COBE.

ISRAELS PLADS

To provide Copenhagen's public with more outdoor spaces, the new Israel Plads transformed a carpark, relocating the parking lot to a subterranean complex and creating a vast plaza and sports park (previous page) on street level. The space acts as a bridge between the urban and the neighboring parkland (above) and provides activity and meeting spaces that cater to all ages (opposite).

THE HOUSE WHERE PLANTS TAKE OVER

TSURUOKA HOUSE
KIYOAKI TAKEDA ARCHITECTS
TOKYO, JAPAN

The supportive structure of Tsuruoka House in Tokyo, Japan, was envisioned to expand the potential of architecture beyond shelter for human life alone, allowing plants to flourish, rather than simply coexist alongside us. The waterfront dwelling was designed by Kiyoaki Takeda Architects, and addresses today's alarming environmental state in which human-made materials have surpassed all living biomass. "Tsuruoka House is an architecture that attempts to hold not only people but also other life forms," says Takeda.

Tsuruoka House subverts the binary of house and garden, merging the two in a stacked and vaulted concrete and steel structure built to support plant life by providing irrigation, fertile garden beds, and supportive trestles. Today, greenery spills from the soil-filled balconies, but the intention is that one day, the garden will become a micro-environment in itself. "Over time, the plants will grow, and birds and insects will introduce unplanned species. Eventually, a small forest could appear," explain the architects. "Then, after decades, existing life forms will grow and hide the building entirely, and ultimately, their biomass must surpass the mass of human-made architecture."

To ensure this, the architecture firm designed vaulted slabs to act as deep, self-draining planters—clear rainwater drainage being essential to the process of supporting other forms of living inhabitants. The shape of these slabs is itself inspired by the flow of water, meaning that the densely packed soil is able to expel excess water with ease. "The thickness of the soil was plotted as deep as possible so that the layered garden would be a small forest hosting a mixture of ground cover plants, shrubs, and small trees," explain the architects. "By opening the garden to other available life forms, providing them with a place to inhabit, and co-creating the community, the garden becomes an 'environment.'"

Following the synchronized scope of the project, the soil and vaulting do not only benefit plant life. The thick soil furnishes the structure with thermal insulation, creating a cool, cave-like refuge in the summer, and what the architects call a "snuggly place" in winter, when the soil traps the warmth from the underfloor heating and gradually releases it. The house is a hopeful blueprint for coexistence. "By respecting supply and demand among all beings in every direction, architecture could be a link to harmonize everyone's role in existence," explains Takeda.

TSURUOKA HOUSE

Tsuruoka House is an ambitious residence that seeks to mutually provide for both human and plant life. The stacked, vaulted levels (page 108 and below) act as deep soil-filled planters for the abundant greenery, which one day will cover the entirety of the building. Meanwhile, on the inside, the arches create cozy, characterful living spaces (opposite).

A BLOOMING VISION FOR URBAN HEALTHCARE

VILLA M

TRIPTYQUE + COLOCO + PHILIPPE STARCK

PARIS, FRANCE

Villa M is a dynamic healthcare-focused center in Paris, France, that addresses the current—and future—need for accessible care in the densely populated city. Located in Montparnasse, the 15th arrondissement, the center was commissioned by healthcare-worker insurance provider Groupe Pasteur Mutualité, and engaged the skills of French-Brazilian firm Triptyque, multidisciplinary studio Coloco (for landscape design), and art director Philippe Starck. "Villa M aims to create a new pact between cities, nature and health," explain the project's heads.

Here, architecture is truly in service of nature, which in turn fosters wellbeing. The radical design envisions the structure as the buttress for the vertical garden facade, the design's leading element. "The building itself is the support for this vertical garden, which will grow and occupy the entire facade, turning the building into a vertical, medicinal forest and becoming the main architecture," explains Triptyque partner, Guillaume Sibaud. The building's prefabricated metal structure is lightweight and simple, arranged in grid-formation to support the plant life. It functions, in essence as a wire mesh, and according to the architects, references early 19th-century Parisian architecture. Coloco's team of landscapers, urban planners, botanists, and gardeners worked to include plants spanning medicinal herbs, fruit trees, and moderately sized perennials that will thrive in the Parisian context, and in time, "become" the facade itself.

The architectural program is broad and envelope-pushing, housing various services under one roof that combine public health with research and the hospitality sector. "The mixed-use complex holds a hotel, restaurant, bar, conference area, check-up area, coworking space, and a showroom for start-ups in the world of health to promote mixing, exchanges, and mutual aid between the different specialties and the different generations of health professionals," explain the architects.

The experimental design is a timely example of dynamic, accessible healthcare that can be spread throughout urban centers, easing the burden on state hospitals and "creating a more open relationship between citizens and health professionals." Designed before the onset of Covid-19, Villa M's revolutionary program "catalyzes the idea of opening healthcare to the city and the city to healthcare," say the architects.

A YOUTH CLUB BUILT FOR FUTURES

CLUB DE NIÑOS Y NIÑAS
CENTRO DE COLABORACIÓN ARQUITECTÓNICA
GREATER MEXICO CITY, MEXICO

The Club de Niños y Niñas (Boys and Girls Club) is a recreational space positively influencing children in an impoverished region of Mexico. The club is located on the border between Tecámac and Ecatepec de Morelos, which has among "the highest population density, insecurity, and crime levels [in Mexico State]," say the architects, and sits within a special crime-prevention zone set up by the federal interior ministry. Designed by Centro de Colaboración Arquitectónica (CCA), the club intends to tackle inequality by providing "young people aged between six and 18 years old a safe and healthy environment for creative, innovative, physical, and intellectual after-school activities," explain the architects. "This is a space that promotes positive values and community integration through play, art, and learning." To engage the community, during the construction process locals were invited to learn more about the mission and partake in the programs on offer.

The expansive club consists of three main buildings with outdoor areas. Building A is an educational zone with classrooms, spaces for music, art and computers, a kitchen, library, and multipurpose space. Built on one level, its windows to the interior courtyards provide ample light and ventilation and negate the need for external windows. This means the building is safeguarded against vandalism; it also prevents students from being distracted by views to the outdoor areas.

Building B is the arts building, hosting exhibitions, dances classes, and educational talks. It also contains a dedicated space where teenagers can relax in a safe environment. Building C, meanwhile, is a high-ceilinged gym-like space for activities and sports with a saw-toothed roof that illuminates the north-facing building. The buildings are interconnected by the club's backbone, a covered, arched-concrete corridor. "Each of the 24 modules represents a human vertebra reflecting the idea that comprehensive education and training is the foundation for a better future," says CCA.

CLUB DE NIÑOS Y NIÑAS

Club de Niños y Niñas is an after-school recreational space built to enrich the lives of at-risk young Mexicans. The complex's three main buildings are connected via an arched concrete corridor (previous page and opposite, bottom right). Light floods from the saw-toothed roof into the interior sports courts (above), while outside, children can play freely and safely in an enclosed courtyard area (opposite, top).

WHERE ELEPHANTS AND HUMANS THRIVE

ELEPHANT WORLD CULTURAL COURTYARD
BANGKOK PROJECT STUDIO
SURIN, THAILAND

The Cultural Courtyard in Surin, Thailand, allows the indigenous Kui people to coexist with the local elephant population. The Kui have lived in harmony with elephants for centuries, but commercial deforestation has caused droughts, food shortages, and the loss of traditional medicinal plants in the area, with devastating consequences for humans, animals, and wildlife. Designed by Bangkok Project Studio, the courtyard is part of Elephant World, "a governmental project to bring the Kui and their elephants back to their homeland and ensure suitable living conditions." Included in the project is the Kui village, an elephant hospital, a preexisting temple and graveyard for humans and elephants, and a museum of Kui culture.

The space's low-lying, pavilion-style structure is built around an open courtyard where events and ceremonies can be held for humans and elephants. Under the 70 × 100 m (230 × 328 ft) sloping roof, six undulating mounds, fitted with concrete seating for 800 people, create a sheltered amphitheater, with one side left open for elephants to enter. The roof contains square openings for cooling ventilation and future plant space: ground-level tree saps will grow to provide extra shade and food for the elephants.

The use of sustainable local materials will make a significant ongoing contribution to the wellbeing of the Kui people and their elephants. The amphitheater mounds are made of soil excavated on site during the creation of a rainwater pond for the animals. Their structure is strengthened by basalt rocks that were mined locally. These were extracted at groundwater level, with the dual benefit of creating a much-needed water reservoir in the neighboring district.

"Moisture has returned to the barren land," explain the architects of the communal turning point the project has heralded. "The Kui can now care for the newly planted trees, maintain the water sources and revive the forest."

The Elephant World Cultural Studio allows the indigenous Kui community in Thailand to once again peacefully coexist with elephants. A pavilion-style building rings an open, ceremonial courtyard (opposite, top) for humans and elephants alike. Mounds of earth covered with local basalt (previous pages), a byproduct of excavating the site to create a rainwater pond (above), sit under the roof and house concrete seating for spectators.

COMMUNITY BUILDING, BRICK BY BRICK

GALLERY HOUSE
ABIN DESIGN STUDIO
MITHAPUKUR, INDIA

Gallery House in Bansberia in West Bengal, India, welcomes its community. The site's owner, who lives across the road, originally commissioned architects Abin Design Studio (ADS) to design a private garage with an upper-level for staff quarters. But ADS saw greater potential for the project, imagining a space for hosting various social and communal activities. Inspired by the proposal, the client let go of the original design in favor of an altruistic build that would dedicate the entire 330 m² (3,552 ft²) space to the public. "The client enjoys a sense of pride and joy of ownership seeing the space put to good use," shares ADS.

Today, the ground floor houses a community hall, while the upper floor offers a sitting area, kitchen, and bathroom facilities. By day, the utilitarian area is used as a tuition space and yoga studio; by night, as a staff dormitory. Structurally, the building employs fluid cutouts where the interiors and exterior blur. This gentle demarcation is a "humane gesture of giving back to the local community, without disrupting the privacy and security of inner functions," explain the architects. Two of the large cutouts form arched entryways to greet visitors: a small, street-level one, and a bigger one, reached by wide steps, offering a vantage point into the foyer.

"Its design was conceived to extend into the street, both visually and physically," explains ADS. The steps also serve as a community gathering place, hosting a streetside gallery during a local annual festival that winds through the neighborhood. Gallery House's facade references its community, too, drawing on West Bengal's long history of ceramic craftsmanship. The intricate design of the exposed brick walls inlaid with ceramic blocks was made in collaboration with a local artist, a homage to West Bengal's terracotta temples. The materials have also been sourced from the surroundings: the ceramic blocks are upcycled industrial seconds and the bricks hail from a nearby riverside brick field.

Gallery House is a mixed-use space designed to benefit its local community in West Bengal, India. Inside and out, the structure reflects local craftsmanship with its intricate masonry that pays homage to the region's terracotta temples. Open at street level via wide stairs that double as public seating (page 112), the fluid layout leads to a spacious community hall (opposite, top).

A GEM-LIKE GALLERY, OPEN TO THE PUBLIC

RUBY CITY CONTEMPORARY ART CENTER
ADJAYE ASSOCIATES
SAN ANTONIO, TEXAS, USA

Designed by Sir David Adjaye, the Ruby City Contemporary Art Center is a contemporary museum built to enrich San Antonio's community with exhibition spaces and art displays. It was the wish of the late patron, Linda Pace, a collector, philanthropist, and artist to provide "a space for the city's thriving creative community to experience works by both local and internationally acclaimed artists," explains the architect's studio, Adjaye Associates. As such, in the roughly 1,300 m² (14,000 ft²) building, a sweeping 929 m² (10,000 ft²) are dedicated to exhibition space alone, featuring Pace's extensive mixed-media collection of over 800 paintings, sculptures, installations, and video works. The art center is part of a wider architectural program encompassing "Chris Park, a one-acre public green space named in memory of Pace's son, and Studio, an auxiliary exhibition space that presents curated shows and programming throughout the year," explains the studio.

The interior's floor plan gently encourages discovery. "The building is conceived to be experienced as an ambulatory loop: from the ground, up and through the independent gallery rooms, and back down returning to the lobby and plaza," says the studio.

Then, there is the art center's striking form, which, when observed from the outside, is an artwork itself. The paneled shell of the angular structure was cast in concrete in Mexico, and colored a decidedly Texan, rich, dusty red. As the eye is drawn up, the texture changes. "For the first 10ft [3 m] up, the concrete is a polished finish, ground to be touched smoothly by a passerby; above, the concrete wall is rough, sharp, and encrusted with two hues of red glass," say Adjaye Associates.

The facade is minimal, interrupted only by a few windows—one that delicately pops out, as if crafted by origami—and the roof grates. "The exterior form consists of a 'heavier' top with sloping soffits, emphasizing its upward lift, topped with two crowning lanterns that create an animated roofline," explains the studio. The asymmetrical form, though commanding, is intended to interact with its surroundings. "The lanterns, in turn, bring natural light into gallery spaces, when desired, and coupled with the two lenses facing Chris Park and San Pedro Creek, respectively, reintroduce views back to the exterior and San Antonio at large." The result is an inviting museum that enlivens both its location and the lives of those that reside close by.

RUBY CITY
CONTEMPORARY ART CENTER

San Antonio's Ruby City Contemporary Art Center is an art object in itself. Its geometric form is made up of a cast-in-concrete shell colored a dusty, Texan red. Mixed with red glass, the facade is polished smooth on ground level, gaining texture as it ascends (opposite, bottom left). The gallery is surrounded by a contrastingly verdant garden (above), which may be viewed, from the interior, via the large glazing.

RUBY CITY

How Can You Build a Community?

Communities cannot be created. Yet, when approached thoughtfully, the architecture of public spaces can help nurture them into existence

Architecture's impact far exceeds the period it was initially destined for, its tangible repercussions reverberating for generations to come. While offering solutions for the future, architecture stands as evidence of the needs of, and challenges faced by, a society at a specific moment in time. As our fast-paced, tormented, and evolving world faces rapid transformations, and societies around the globe acknowledge the ineptitude of current living conditions and systems, we find ourselves in need of a new "spatial contract"—a way of living, encompassing social, economic, and political dimensions. New challenges require new approaches, and, in the words of Lebanese architect Hashim Sarkis, "problems such as racial segregation in cities, gender inequalities, coastal flooding, social mobility, and material scarcity [demand] new epistemologies."[1]

The multifunctional Herstedlund Community Center (above and top).

While awareness of this issue has grown, the accumulation of these factors coupled with worldwide health, climate, and social emergencies has changed the paradigms and shifted the general consensus surrounding architecture's function. Where once it was enough to recognize issues and reflect upon solutions, many are now taking a more radical position that refuses to tolerate negligence and establishes these matters as the focal point of all design strategies. Novel ways of occupying fundamental spaces are emerging everyday. Notions like sustainability, affordability, and inclusivity are being considered, while architectural projects are drifting increasingly beyond mono-functionality. Nature has been reintroduced to our cities and to our homes, and residents have established a fresh appreciation of the outdoors. In addition, a new lexicon has appeared, encompassing words like "coworking," "biophilia," and "social infrastructure." Other terms, such as "spatial experience," "resilience," and "shared spaces," have taken on more elaborate meanings, and recent projects have advertised ambitious plans for "building communities." But what is a community, really? And how can you actually create one?

A community is a group of people sharing common characteristics that allow them to live cohesively within a given space. Practicing collective ownership of the public realm, individuals in this type of consortium have similar social perceptions that consequently conjure up a sense of solidarity. While our urban entities become more diverse, and as cities draw different groups of people from multiple backgrounds with distinct world-views, our understanding of community must expand to distinguish what brings us together, rather than what drives us apart. That said, a community cannot be created but instead must be developed over time by establishing social connection and trust.

Cities—or as the Ghanaian-Scottish architect and curator of the 2023 Venice Architecture Biennale, Lesley Lokko, describes them, "places where we meet people who are not like us"[2]—present economic opportunities while nurturing social divisions and inequalities. To quote the Spanish architect Carlos García Vázquez, "People came to find freedom, anonymity, and opportunities ... and for it got loneliness, instability, confusion, and a loss of identity."[3] Contrary to some radical ideologies, the diversity found in urban agglomerations can help enrich the way we live, and the first step towards this objective is questioning how to create a civic society. Since people from different backgrounds have different interpretations of the same concept, relevant definitions should be agreed upon, because what is considered public for some could mean the opposite for others. In fact, "how can you be in a city if you have never been in a city?" asks Lokko. "We cannot assume that people know how to be in a city and know how to integrate."[4] It is only through involving individuals, understanding all components, and enhancing connections that people can become citizens, thereby drafting a system of values that will inform and shape the culture of a city.

Designed as a giant exhibition, Superkilen is dotted with everyday objects (above) representing the 60 nationalities of the area's local residents.

Superkilen (above) occupies a 750 m (2,460 ft) stretch of Copenhagen's Nørrebro district; one of Denmark's most multi-ethnic yet poor neighborhoods.

Social interactions, chance encounters, and unplanned activities can be encouraged by design. As American architect and planner Denise Scott Brown once said, "Architecture can't force people to connect [but] it can ... plan the crossing points, remove barriers, and make the meeting places useful and attractive."[5] "Reimagining the Civic Commons," Studio Gang's booklet of seven strategies to help communities reimagine and activate their public and accessible spaces, is a good example of this. In Denmark, meanwhile, Dorte Mandrup's Herstedlund Community Center has imagined a framework of joint activities in a family-oriented residential area. The center's open program is designed to spark interaction and can be expanded to provide new spaces that cater to different age groups and communities. With the Peach Hut Community Center, China's Atelier Xi generated the first in a series of independent miniature facilities to better serve rural communities, expanding upon the project's original brief which requested one large, principal site.

Cities are for people, and their public spaces are the principal arena for the creation of human connections. Since the start of the Covid-19 pandemic, public and open spaces have gained additional relevance. A collective appropriation of this public realm, as well as the incorporation of various new usages within it, have occurred on a global scale. As our first point of contact with a city, public spaces embody freedom of movement and of expression. Open, free, and accessible to all, these areas do not belong to specific people and are not exclusive to certain groups. As such, they are in fact given meaning only through their communal uses.

Ranging from planned streets, intersections, plazas, boulevards, parks, and squares, to informal sidewalk settings,

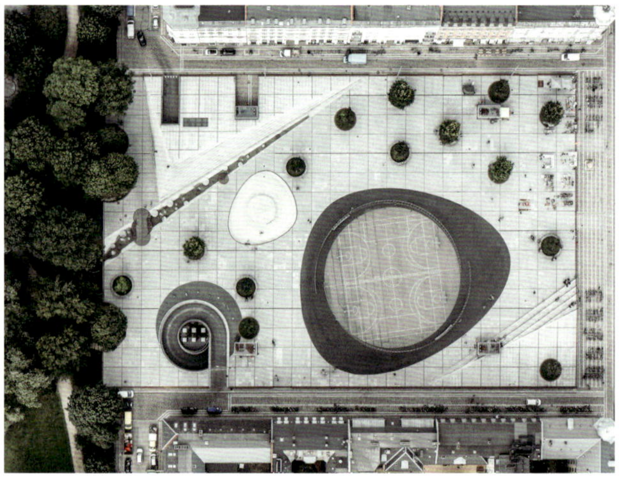

Peach Hut Community Center (above, top) serves rural communities in China.

Israels Plads (above, bottom) is a diverse and dynamic plaza in Denmark.

Miyashita Park (above), a new model for urban relaxation and activation.

interstitial spaces, and an overflow of private spaces into the public domain, public spaces have many roles. In Copenhagen, Topotek 1, BIG, and Superflex collaborated to create Superkilen, a half-mile-long urban stretch in one of the most ethnically diverse and socially challenged neighborhoods in Denmark. Encouraging the urban practices of 60 different nationalities, the space is an open exhibition that introduces each of these cultures. To enhance a sense of belonging, public spaces need to cater to different groups of people, across different kinds of sites. In Copenhagen, COBE reimagined Israels Plads as a vibrant and diverse plaza for leisure, sport, culture, and public events. Situated atop an underground car park, it also creates a smooth transition between the urban environment and a neighboring park. In Japan, conversely, dense urban agglomerations have resulted in the creation of vertical facilities that encompass multiple functions. Miyashita

Park by Nikken Sekkei, for instance, combines a public park with commercial and hospitality spaces, demonstrating new possibilities for public spaces.

As these comments illustrate, while societies in every era face varying challenges, architecture is uniquely positioned as a discipline to solve some of humanity's greatest logistical and communal quandaries. Designers and builders have major responsibilities that span their lifetimes, and impact future generations to come. For instance, the high architecture principles of yesterday have today fostered our consumer-oriented society and all the collateral damage that has spawned. As generators of new models, architects can imagine alternative forms of living, but ultimately it is the community that must implement them. As the world faces greater separation, widening political divisions, and growing economic inequalities, architects must look, first and foremost, to people to shape the architecture of public spaces, while citizens, in turn, must come together in a spirit of collaboration to bring these designs to life.

Notions like sustainability, affordability, and inclusivity are being considered, while architectural projects are drifting increasingly beyond mono-functionality.

Green Square Library (above), a generous urban living room.

Green Square Library (above) and Place of Remembrance (top) provide inviting, meditative spaces for communities in Sydney and Lima respectively.

GOOD ARCHITECTURE IS INNOVATIVE

Innovative architecture breaks new boundaries, simultaneously drawing on the past to reimagine the future

When looking at a list of synonyms for "innovative," one often finds terms conveying ideas of newness and novelty. And while a certain up-to-date quality is indeed inherent to innovation, what these lists often disregard is the fact that innovative can also mean the use of old ways of thinking, or previously established techniques, in unfamiliar ways.

This is as true of architecture as it is elsewhere. In a discipline that is so intrinsically linked to human evolution, and which simultaneously produces structures that are meant to stand the test of time, it is only natural that innovative buildings look to the past in order to realign boundaries for the future. To ensure better places for life's many facets—now and always—architects and designers must constantly anticipate cultural shifts and environmental changes, as well as question the very idea of what makes a building good.

The projects in this chapter are exemplary cases of designs that are not just good, but often paradigm-shifting in their physical embodiment of such forward-thinking. From their mind-bogglingly imaginative forms to their demonstration of bold technical advancements or unexpected materials choices, the buildings outlined as part of this principle are all the facets of innovation-made-real within different environments across the globe.

One such facet is the idea of innovative architecture being inspiring. Not just to other architects, but to the general public, too. Often, this is intimately connected to a building's form and first impression within its physical context, but this principle also extends to its use and cultural significance. This is as true for the ancient Egyptian pyramids as it is for the revolutionary designs of Thomas Jefferson, Eileen Gray, and Francis Kéré. When the shape of a building seems to defy the laws of physics, fuels its community, or fuses utopia with pragmatism—that's when it inspires discussion, competition, and wonder.

Another facet of innovation, often connected to the immediate physical appearance of a built structure, is a certain visionary quality on the part of its architect(s). For example, it is due to the magnificent imaginations of Antoni Gaudí, Frank Gehry, and Carme Pigem that we can now feast our eyes on La Sagrada Familia, Bilbao's Guggenheim, and the Soulages Museum. Again, the canon of architecture reverberates throughout history in such innovative structures, and those featured in the following remarks will hopefully join them. By employing known shapes, surfaces, or materials in unexpected ways, visionary architects raise fundamental questions about who we are and where we're going.

And when it comes to innovative architecture, the issue of materials is always important. To pioneer or experiment with a material is to pave the way for future exploration; it is to be at the forefront of issues spanning supply chains, sustainability, engineering, and culture. While concrete still constitutes a vast majority of our built environment—and has been molded into truly astounding shapes in the hands of Zaha Hadid or Tadao Ando—local, renewable, and adaptable materials are the future. Once more, a look to the past can help redefine what's possible going forward. Qasab reed, a tall grass similar to bamboo, has been employed by the Mad'an community of Iraq for thousands of years to construct houses in as little as three days, and is a powerful case study not just for building *with* (rather than *on*) nature, but for decolonizing the way we look at architecture and innovation as a whole. Through the inclusion or pioneering of unexpected materials, buildings designed for the future can help address existential challenges like climate change. They can also bridge the ever-increasing gaps between cultures through a philosophy of dialogue and accountability.

The facet of innovative architecture that may be most obviously related to the quality of newness is that of technology. As science and knowledge evolve, so do building technologies. Projects may be planned years before the engineering power needed to realize them actually exists (like New York City's Hudson Yards) or include complex energy, waste, and air systems to comply with standards of climate efficiency and sustainability. High technologies afford a creative freedom to architects of the present and future that may seem hard to live without. However, new ways of including old, even ancient, technologies (like the towering windcatchers of ancient Persia or Bali's sacred rice terraces) provide an equally reliable source of innovation that is exemplified in the buildings this section introduces.

What all of them show is that innovative architecture takes into consideration not just its own lifetime by being inspiring, radical, experimental, or technologically advanced, but will—in the very best of cases—transcend ages with a unique mosaic of these boundary-pushing qualities.

AT HOME IN A SANDSTONE CAVE

CA'N TERRA

ENSAMBLE STUDIO

MENORCA, SPAIN

Hewn from a cave, Ca'n Terra (Home in the Earth in Catalan) is a home that honors Menorca's history. Converted into a holiday home by the architect couple behind Ensamble Studio, in its former life it was a quarry for Marés stone, Menorca's sandstone. Later, during the Spanish Civil War, it was used as an ammunition dump, before being rediscovered by the architects. "The found space has industrial logic, artistic potential as a sublime cavern carved by hand, and mineral nature as an extract of the stony landscape on the island of Menorca," the architects explain. "Finding this excavated space in the guts of the earth and reinventing its use implies writing a new story that can rescue it from its abandonment."

This faithfulness to the space saw the architects take a sensitive approach with minimal intervention, allowing what was there to inform this new iteration. "In lieu of the imposing action that we often exert on the environment, we propose a trip to the interior being of matter, and recognize the beauty of the spaces that are waiting to be lived," explain the duo. "This is a project that boldly seeks a balance between nature and artifice, between histories and times, between people and the environment."

Scanning the space with laser technology to inform their decisions, the architects added subtle structure with precast slabs made of cement mixed with the site's Marés stone powder. The intervention follows the natural topography, and the free-flowing layout remains otherwise nonhierarchical. Light and ventilation was brought in by carving three skylights into the darker recesses of the cave, while translucent panels act as windows to the exterior.

To turn the cave into a functioning shelter, it was fitted with solar panels, a septic tank, a water cistern, and a swimming pool that repurposes part of the excavated space. The cave was swept clean of mold and dirt but otherwise retains its raw eathern look inside, as if its inhabitants just happened to move in.

Ca'n Terra is a naturalistic holiday home housed within a Menorcan cave. To retain its character, the architects intervened minimally, leaving the surfaces as they found them, and only gently reinforcing the existing layout with added walls made of cement and local marés stone (previous page, top, and opposite, top). Light was brought in with skylights and transparent sheets in lieu of windows (opposite and above).

Pictured from above, the only sign of human intervention to the cave complex is a string of solar panels (opposite, top). Inside and out, the project respects the presence of the pre-existing nature (opposite, bottom). One of few added features is the generous swimming pool that occupies an excavated space in the cave (above).

AN INVISIBLE BRIDGE, FIT FOR A FORTRESS

MOSES BRIDGE
RO&AD ARCHITECTEN
HALSTEREN, NETHERLANDS

On first sight, the Moses Bridge appears to be an optical illusion, sunk into water, yet completely watertight. Designed by RO&AD Architecten, it is in fact an extraordinary feat of engineering. The "invisible" bridge forms part of a historic restoration of the West Brabant Defense Line, a 17th-century defense strategy that protected cities and villages with fortresses and walls. In its heyday, the northeastern portion could link up with the area's natural waterways to tactically inundate land and transform this region of the Netherlands into an island. In the 19th century, the waterline fell into disrepair, but has been recently restored, forming part of various public leisure roots for cycling and hiking.

A walkway was needed to ferry visitors across the moat of Fort de Roovere, the largest of the forts on the line. Yet the brief was a historically sensitive one; after all, a fort connected from land to land via bridge is strategically weak. "It is, of course, highly improper to build bridges across the moats of defense works, especially on the side of the fortress the enemy was expected to appear on. That's why we designed an 'invisible' bridge," RO&AD explains.

The bridge structure follows the line of the landscape, sitting flush with the soil and the water level. It is accessed by staircases that cut cleanly through the grassy bank on one side and the steep fortress embankment on the other. "The bridge can't be seen from a distance because the ground and the water come all the way up to its edge. When you get closer, the fortress opens up to you through a narrow trench. You can then walk up to its gates like Moses on the water," the architects suggest, discussing the inspiration behind their miracle-emulating concept.

The bridge's hardwood deck and stairs are made entirely of durable Accoya wood that has been waterproofed with EPDM foil. The wood is manufactured to avoid swelling and shrinking and contains an anti-fungal coating that prevents it from degrading. As they traverse the bridge, visitors are almost eye-to-eye with the water, but remain safely dry. The bridge's walls sit perfectly at the water line thanks to adjustable dams on each side that control water levels, while a pump under the bridge drains rain water and any overflow. The bridge continues to attract visitors to the restored area, who marvel at its novel design, skimming their hands over the surface water as they walk—almost upon it.

THE HOUSE THAT 3D PRINTING BUILT

TECLA HOUSE

MARIO CUCINELLA ARCHITECTS + WASP

MASSA LOMBARDA, ITALY

The prototype TECLA (short for technology and clay) is the first ever sustainable, 3D-printed housing structure made from local raw earth. Built in Massa Lombarda, Italy, the project draws on the eco-sustainability research of the SOS – School of Sustainability. A training center founded by Mario Cucinella, the school worked alongside the designer's own studio, as well as Italian 3D-printing practice WASP, to create the site. Their aim was to address the climate emergency and the need for sustainable homes in the face of large-scale migration and natural disasters.

The concept of the build unites the earthen, rounded features of ancient homes with pioneering 21st-century technology. "TECLA is an innovative circular housing model that brings together research on vernacular construction practices, the study of bioclimatic principles, and the use of natural and local materials," Mario Cucinella Architects explains. "It is a nearly zero-emission project: its casing and the use of an entirely local material allows for the reduction of waste and scraps. This and the use of raw earth makes TECLA a pioneering example of low-carbon housing."

The creation of TECLA took 200 hours of printing and 60 m^3 (2,119 ft^3) of natural materials, but an average consumption of less than 6kW. The shape of the 60 m^2 (646 ft^2) building follows a balanced, structurally robust sine curve, made up of two circular spaces. One contains a kitchen and living area, the other a sleeping area, connected by a passageway. The building's material and its shape are optimized for the local climate and balance thermal mass, insulation, and ventilation.

The project saw the successful implementation of the revolutionary Crane WASP, the first 3D printer that is both modular and multilevel. "We like to think that TECLA is the beginning of a new story," added Mario Cucinella founder and creative director of Mario Cucinella Architects. "It would be truly extraordinary to shape the future by transforming this ancient material with the technologies we have available today."

A BAMBOO PAVILION AHEAD OF THE CURVE

THE ARC AT GREEN SCHOOL

IBUKU

ABIANSEMAL, INDONESIA

The Arc is an open-air sport, leisure, and community space built entirely of bamboo. Its shingled, undulating rooftop almost sweeps the ground, protecting those inside from the elements, and seems to resemble a resting armored pangolin or slumbering giant tortoise. The building was designed by Bali-based studio IBUKU, whose practice is dedicated to innovative naturalistic architecture, and was commissioned by the sustainability-focused Green School in Bali. According to IBUKU, it is "an unprecedented structure which is not only an incredible piece of bamboo architecture, but will serve as a reference in lightweight structures altogether."

The pavilion-style building required true feats of engineering to achieve. The structure's framework is a series of intersecting 14 m (46 ft) bamboo arches each spanning 19 m (62 ft) that are reinforced by "gridshells" that curve in opposite directions to form solid support throughout. "The Arc's counterintuitive orchestration of geometry brings the structure into a state of equilibrium, which means a dramatically decreased necessity for structural material," IBUKU explains. Encased within the thin structure, the interior space is maximized with no need for, what the architects call, "distracting" supporting trusses.

For inspiration, IBUKU looked inward. "The Arc employs one of nature's greatest strategies for creating large spaces with minimal structure. Within a human ribcage, a series of ribs working in compression are held in place by a tensioned flexible layer of muscle and skin. This creates a thin but strong encasement for the lungs," explains IBUKU. "In the case of The Arc, arches working in compression are held in place by tensioned anticlastic gridshells. These fields of gridshells appear to drape across the spaces between impossibly thin arches soaring overhead, giving a whimsy, intimacy, and beauty to the space. Although the gridshells appear to hang from the arches, they actually hold them up."

THE ARC AT GREEN SCHOOL

Built entirely of bamboo, The Arc at Green School is an innovative sport, leisure, and community space.

The pavilion's undulating, bamboo-shingled roof (opposite, bottom) almost sweeps the ground (previous page), protecting the inside from the tropical elements and allowing for cooling ventilation.

Materials Stimulating Good Architecture

From ultra-thin concrete and mass timber to 3D printing and digital manufacturing, a host of new materials and technologies are shaping building's future

What materials should we choose? From aesthetics to ethics, the specification of appropriate materials is one of the biggest responsibilities currently facing architects, and our understanding of them needs to extend beyond the formal and the functional. Today, our design decisions must be guided by the environmental impact of materials at each stage of their life cycle, and the industry is gearing up to respond to these requirements.

The built environment, and each one of its material components, exerts significant pressure on global natural resources, contributing, inevitably, to greenhouse gas emissions. According to the "2021 Global Status Report for Buildings and Construction," the construction sector accounts for 37 percent of CO_2 emissions. Elsewhere, this study also suggests that, by 2060, the use of materials is likely to double, and, according to the Office for Economic Co-operation and Development (OECD), by the same year concrete alone will produce 12 percent of all greenhouse gas emissions.

ETH Zurich's Armadillo Vault (above), a stone canopy fused by compression.

Traditional materials are now being reinvented to maximize their intrinsic qualities and adapted to meet modern environmental requirements. Concrete, one of the world's most utilized materials, accounts for the production of more than four billion metric tons of cement each year.[1] Many major works of modern architecture have been fashioned from this material, yet its environmental impact is enormous.

To reduce its contribution to greenhouse emissions, the building-materials industry is developing new types of concrete that are moving in the direction of carbon neutrality. In 2020, LafargeHolcim launched ECOPact, a concrete that is capable of generating "from 30 percent to 100 percent less carbon emissions compared to standard concrete."[2] And the DB Group has developed Cemfree, a cement-free concrete that can save up to 80 percent in embodied CO_2.[3]

Architects are not far behind in this endeavor: a group of researchers at ETH Zurich, along with the architecture firm Supermanoeuvre, have created an innovative formwork system consisting of a net of steel cables and polymer fabric stretched into a reusable scaffolding structure. This system can produce ultra-thin, self-supporting concrete roof systems with an average thickness of just 5 cm (1.97 in). Another firm, Hyperion Robotics, has partnered with the Peikko Group to use 3D printing with low-carbon concrete to manufacture structural foundations, reducing the amount of concrete required by up to 75 percent, as well as the volume of waste. In both cases, manufacturing technology and digital design have made it possible to minimize the amount of material needed.

At the same time, mass timber is expanding the possibilities of wood's role in construction. With regulations regarding sustainable harvesting growing ever stricter, timber products offer an attractive alternative to the mass use of concrete and steel. Unlike these materials, wood from controlled forestry stores carbon rather than emitting it, as trees feed on CO_2 as they grow. Consequently, although timber harvesting and manufacturing require high levels of energy, it will never surpass the amount of carbon sequestered.[4]

Matching the structural capability of reinforced concrete, but offering greater flexibility and deformation resistance, mass timber is leading the way in the race to replace concrete in large-scale construction. Mass timber, which counts cross-laminated timber, glued-laminated timber, and nail-laminated timber among its major exponents, is created by binding pieces of wood together to create large-scale

In Switzerland, the Block Research Group made a lightweight, ultra-thin, curved concrete roof (above, both) for the NEST building's HiLo Unit.

The Spheres, Seattle (opposite, top), made with ECOPlanet green cement. A 3D-printed concrete bridge (above, both) by Zaha Hadid Architects and ETH Zurich.

structural elements such as beams, pillars, and panels for walls and floors. By using different types of mass timber, it is possible to construct buildings up to 18-stories high,[5] examples of which are beginning to crop up among city skylines, offering housing that is highly efficient and can also save on heating and cooling.

In this respect, such new technologies have not only made it possible to reinvent traditional materials, but have also sparked the emergence of a groundbreaking range of systems, techniques, and new materials. Tools such as building information modeling, virtual and augmented reality, and digital manufacturing, among others, have begun to blur the boundaries between design and construction, and the role of materials is changing with them. Today, it is possible to coordinate multiple disciplines simultaneously, prefabricating complete systems that enable buildings to be assembled from kits of parts, increasing speed and precision and reducing errors, manpower, and overall budget. For example, computer numerical control makes it possible to machine timber beams and panels to create precise components according to a series of coordinates, which can then be efficiently joined using fastening systems.

Also known as additive manufacturing, 3D printing is changing the paradigm within the construction industry, making it possible to manufacture objects and architectural elements through the addition of layered materials, following a predesigned model. There are printers so large that it is possible to construct entire dwellings in situ, and the power of this breakthrough technology is such that, by 2025, Dubai is planning to have a quarter of its buildings constructed using 3D-printing methods. It is also expected that between 2021 and 2028, the global 3D-printing market will grow by 91 percent.[6]

Biomaterials are also booming: in addition to reducing extractive processes and introducing a more rustic and natural aesthetic, they are biodegradable at the end of their useful lifespans. For instance, some biomaterials, such as hempcrete, not only sequester carbon emissions as they grow but during the lifetime of the building as well. Many of them are compatible with the new digital technologies—for example, 3D printing with raw earth, sand, and even agricultural waste.[7]

TECLA (above, both) is the first eco-sustainable housing model. Conceived by Mario Cucinella Architects, it was 3D-printed from local raw earth.

The HiLo's roof was built using a cable-net and fabric formwork (above).

Given the gravity of the climate emergency, we need to embrace a circular built environment, and these pioneering efforts in the industry appear to be well on track. However, mindfulness surrounding the environmental impact of materials and components must be coupled with other effective solutions like the creation of simple, and ideally modular, recyclable systems designed for deconstruction. Similarly, adopting environmentally friendly materials and seeking out local alternatives to replace concrete and steel would have an even greater effect. Finally, according to the "2021 Global Status Report," best-practice architecture should be built with materials that enable a circular economy, making it possible "to keep materials and resources in use as long as possible, and ideally forever, in a closed cycle of extended use, reuse, and recycling."[8]

As Paul Emmons, professor at the Washington-Alexandria Architecture Center of Virginia Tech, has said, "Architects make drawings rather than buildings."[9] Therefore, it is our task to ensure that each of the lines we draw—and the future materials we use—express a real awareness of their effects on the world in which we live.

From aesthetics to ethics, the specification of appropriate materials is one of the biggest responsibilities currently facing architects.

The KnitCandela prototype (above) by Zaha Hadid Architects and ETH Zurich.

A 3D-knitted shell, the KnitCandela (above, both) allows for the construction of lightweight, freeform concrete structures without using molds.

SNØHETTA'S CRAIG DYKERS: A COLLECTIVIST

Bridging the gap across disparate fields, Snøhetta's designs are fueled by collaboration and a set of guiding principles rather than a fixed aesthetic

"Architecture is a living profession, a living art, and a growing science," says Craig Dykers, one of the founding directors of world-renowned architecture studio Snøhetta. "For it to be successful, it must be a part of life, and not restrict itself within the boundaries of its own profession." This is not only Dykers's response to a question about understanding architecture as a balance between art and science, but also an insight into Snøhetta's unique ability to draw inspiration from across a wide variety of disciplines beyond the field of architecture. In 2007, for example, the studio deployed sleight-of-hand and used a ha-ha (sunken fence) instead of railings on the roof of the Oslo Opera House, prompted by similar use in zoo enclosures. Elsewhere, during its 2017 redesign of New York City's Times Square, it drew from noted animal behaviorist Temple Grandin while attempting to improve the area's flow of people.

While such transdisciplinary methods are integral to Snøhetta's design processes, they are perhaps particularly reflective of Dykers's own distinct background. Born in Frankfurt, the son of a U.S. Army corporal,

MADISON

In conceiving the Calgary Library in Canada (above and opposite), Snøhetta first consulted with the local population to discover their needs and desires.

The dynamic design extends over four floors, providing an array of spaces that cater to different kinds of interaction: digital and analog, group and individual. Snøhetta is currently revitalizing 550 Madison Garden in New York—a 1980s, postmodernist icon—incorporating a densely vegetated public garden (previous page).

Dykers spent most of his childhood in Germany. Later in life, while studying pre-med at the University of Texas in Austin, Dykers had a change of heart and decided to jump ship to art instead of medicine. Steered away from art towards architecture by his father, "who felt my interest in both science and art would [make it] more fitting for my temperament," Dykers remains content with his decision some 30 years later. "Architecture allows you to find new expressions and perspectives through a process of discovery," he says. "It also adds the component of human behavior that makes it even more intriguing."

Snøhetta's birth, not long after Dykers's graduation in 1985, is already the stuff of architectural legend. In 1989, aged just 28, Dykers and a group of seven architect friends from Norway and the U.S.—including Kjetil Trædal Thorsen, Snøhetta's other founding partner—entered an anonymous competition to design the Bibliotheca Alexandrina in Egypt: their submission beat more than 500 others. While the win catapulted the practice onto the global stage, working out the project's logistics was also the making of the practice: 14 people from the fledgling studio, with children and families in tow, relocated to Cairo for almost a year and a half. Once embedded, the team finessed the design with a local engineering partner and helped train young stonemasons to carve the massive granite facade with a series of ancient and modern texts, even going so far as to open a quarry. "It was very much hands-on architecture," Thorsen explained in a 2019 interview with *Dezeen*. "We were following every piece of the building, from A–Z, on site." Methods developed while working on their very first project helped shape the hands-on, nonhierarchical, and collectivist approach that Snøhetta has subsequently become known for.

From a team of seven in the late 1980s to 280 members of staff today, spread over two headquarters (in Oslo and New York) and five satellite offices (in Hong Kong, Paris, Innsbruck, Adelaide, and San Francisco), Dykers explains that, despite being dotted across the globe, the collective, collaborative nature of Snøhetta is maintained and nurtured through "an ethos or set of principles that guide us." These guiding principles, Dykers says, "are generally centered upon social, environmental, and economic sustainability. This means that design work can vary but the ethos remains." Such philosophies are how Snøhetta has been able to bring together architects, landscape architects, interior architects, and graphic designers to build a portfolio of projects as varied as the 9/11 Memorial and Museum Pavilion in New York, a pavilion for wild reindeer in the middle of Norway, the aforementioned Oslo Opera House, and a redesign of the Norwegian kroner banknotes.

For Dykers, the advantages of a practice centered around cooperation are numerous and, frankly, obvious. "Many people interact with architecture so it stands to reason that many people should create [architecture]," he says. "This is especially important in our challenging contemporary world. All architecture is collective at some level, even smaller projects require cooperation. The larger the project, the greater the need for interaction and sharing." By way of example, Dykers points to Snøhetta's Calgary Library in Canada. The design team responsible for the project spent considerable time speaking with the local population to better understand the needs, desires, and dreams of those who would eventually use the building. For Dykers, the fact that this on-the-ground work was carried out, enabled the architects to transform these needs and desires into a structure that allows "a wide variety of people to come together to make a place of congregation and energized interaction."

More recently, Snøhetta has been looking to address what Dykers refers to as "climate abuse" through their work—particularly through material choices, how they build, and post-construction impact. Dykers highlights two

Demonstrative of Snøhetta's radically imaginative approach, Under (above) is a sunken restaurant and research center for marine life in Norway. The jutting design pays tribute to the rocky Norwegian coastline. The building's concrete tube shell was built on a nearby barge and then filled with water to part-submerge it. Inside, the restaurant's atmosphere is warm and inviting (opposite). A window offers views of the seabed and, at night, artificial lighting is used to attract fish.

CRAIG DYKERS

projects the practice is currently engaged with that embody questions relating to environmental sustainability: the Theodore Roosevelt Presidential Library in Medora, North Dakota, and the new Ford Motor Company Research & Engineering Campus in Dearborn, Michigan. "Both of these projects work with carbon sequestration using common methods such as managing material use and production lines, as well as limiting energy use," Dykers says, but they also do so through "managing the landscape design through plant and soil characteristics." Yet each of these aspects connect beyond the specific individual site to a wider understanding of habitat in order to stress the broader relationships between nature, landscape, and architecture.

It is Snøhetta's unique ability to unite these disparate fields, combined with its working methods that privilege collectivity and collaboration, that enables the studio to design buildings that are sensitive to their surroundings without adhering to any set aesthetic. Dykers remarks that while the studio has begun to build certain patterns of identity over its 30 years in practice, the idea of a specific aesthetic is not and never has been the primary focus for the creation of new work. Instead, he says, Snøhetta shares "principles and methodologies … to help keep our focus on the values that are important to us." And while aesthetics are important to Snøhetta, in that the studio appreciates the ability of aesthetics to shift and shape people's moods and behavior, they are not necessarily a driving factor. By prioritizing the values that matter, Snøhetta's signature has become, as Dykers says, "a commitment to humanity and the environment that people naturally connect [with] us," rather than any specific expression of form.

"Architecture allows you to find new expressions and perspectives through a process of discovery. It also adds the component of human behavior."

With its walkable, curved roof, the Theodore Roosevelt Presidential Library in North Dakota (opposite, both) blends harmoniously with its mountainous surroundings.

For the Oslo Opera House (above), Snøhetta created a wave-like structure that serves to symbolically connect the ground and water on the Bjørvika Peninsula.

The building prioritizes accessibility, employing a "carpet" of horizontal and sloping surfaces that likewise guides visitors gradually up towards its roof.

A HALF-SUNK RESTAURANT ON THE OCEAN FLOOR

UNDER

SNØHETTA

SPANGEREID, NORWAY

Under is an ambient restaurant and marine research center that appears to be submerged into the stormy Norwegian sea it calls home. The building is located on Norway's southernmost tip, where storms from north and south converge, and the resulting brackish water creates the perfect conditions for marine biodiversity. Under's dual purpose allows visitors to observe their surroundings above and below sea level, while paying "tribute to the wild fauna of the sea and to the rocky coastline of Norway's southern tip," explain the architects, Snøhetta.

The building's outer form—a sunken concrete capsule—mimics its unruly outdoor setting, and is bolted onto a concrete slab that is anchored to the bedrock beneath the seabed. Its shell was built on a barge 20 m (66 ft) from the site, and was floated into the sea by way of a crane and tugboats. "In order to ensure a proper connection to the bolts on the concrete slab, the construction team filled the structure with water to make it sink. After ensuring that all bolts were fully tightened, the water was drained away, allowing the interior work to begin," explains Snøhetta. In contrast to the dramatic exterior, the entrance was modeled as a welcoming refuge.

Snøhetta worked with Hamran, a local carpentry workshop, to employ Norwegian wood to its warmest and most elegant effect. As one moves through the building to the dining areas, the wood shifts to more refined interior accents, with dark raw steel and brass. "As a metaphor for the journey of descent, the color of the textile-clad interior turns darker and more intense the deeper one goes below water," explain the architects. "At the entrance, the ceiling's neutral color deepens into a sunset pink, intense coral, sea green, and finally culminates in a midnight blue as one arrives at the dining room."

The mezzanine bar area is level with the waterline, and boasts a vertical window that extends from above sea level down to the sea bed, framing the elements. "The window reveals the convergence of sea and air, with the volatile waterline dancing to the intensity of the wind," the architects suggest. Then, at the heart of the building is the 40-person dining area, with its large horizontal window like a silver screen out to the seabed. "The view from the window will evolve gradually throughout the day and seasons," they continue, "with the color of the water shifting from sapphire blue during a cold winter day, to emerald green in the summer season, when the algae set in."

Appearing half-sunken off the coast of Norway's southernmost tip (previous page), Under is a dramatic restaurant and marine-research complex. The upper levels, decked with welcoming wooden panels (opposite, bottom left) offer views above and beyond sea-level via a long vertical window, and lead down to an ocean-floor restaurant (opposite, top) where the interiors skew to increasingly moody blues.

GOOD ARCHITECTURE IS LOCAL

Local architecture respects its environment, the history that sustains it, and the lives of its inhabitants, reviving traditional methods to inform new solutions

Over the past few decades, globalization has dramatically influenced the ways in which we design and build our towns and cities, resulting in a sometimes troublesome one-size-fits-all approach. In many respects, this has not only robbed us of a sense of belonging within the built environments we inhabit, but has also resulted in spaces that simply don't meet the requirements of their specific location—from the use of materials unsuited to certain climate conditions to building methods that prioritize style over practicality and durability.

As the climate crisis escalates, and the effects of neoliberalism continue to encourage an individualized, yet hyper-globalized, mode of existence, rooting architecture in its local context is more vital now than ever before. In architectural terms, the word "local" can extend to climate, culture, materiality, and production processes, among other factors, all of which, more often than not, are grounded in a region's history. Reconnecting with the architecture of bygone eras, and the site-specific knowledge this embodies, is the single best way of understanding and conserving the use of local techniques and materials—which often prove the most climate and cost-effective solutions, too.

This preservation and revival of vernacular building methods can simultaneously empower and uplift communities, promoting a sense of autonomy in the creation and management of their architectural surroundings, while bolstering the local economy. As such, this kind of architecture has the potential to be used as a tool for change, triggering advocacy processes through participation and exchange, and prompting a sense of socio-environmental responsibility among citizens. Pairing these inherited forms of knowledge with contemporary technologies and new construction systems can enhance such building methods further, resulting in a contemporary take on traditional architecture that is better equipped to reduce our carbon footprint, as well as to improve the habitability of our built spaces and the quality of life beyond their walls.

Appreciating the nuances of local architecture and its various adaptive processes requires a sharp eye that recognizes the uniqueness of each site, and how its past informs its present. The amount of historic knowledge that goes into creating an adobe brick wall, for instance, would surprise those unfamiliar with this material. Yet the cumulative effect of architecture that understands its context and takes its cues from its surrounding environment, is that, even to the untrained eye, it establishes itself as a cohesive part of a place's cultural fabric. In this way, successful vernacular architecture can cultivate and strengthen a sense of identity and heritage, acknowledging and venerating the local histories that make us who we are.

In this section of the book, you will encounter projects that demonstrate local architecture at its most innovative and effective, ranging from a pioneering use of bamboo to create a restaurant that is at once traditional and trailblazing, and entirely at one with its verdant surroundings, to a school that makes clever new use of regional materials and techniques to dramatically improve the comfort and lifestyle of those it envelops. Elsewhere, an elegant sauna breathes new life into its surroundings while simultaneously paying homage to its site's past, while a recycling venue offers a masterclass in sustainable local techniques, encouraging community participation in the preservation of the area's natural environment.

Good local architecture, then, is one that combines the best of past and present to respond to the climatic, social, and economic conditions of its location, honoring people, place, and cultural heritage while helping to instill a sense of communal pride and responsibility for the lived environments that are so briefly ours.

THE FINNISH PUBLIC SAUNA REVIVED FOR TOMORROW

LÖYLY PUBLIC SAUNA
AVANTO ARCHITECTS
HELSINKI, FINLAND

Löyly, a coastal public sauna, approximately three kilometers (two miles) on foot from Helsinki's city center, is part of a growing movement to keep the social Finnish custom alive, as Finns increasingly favor private saunas in the home. Löyly, its namesake, is the uniquely Finnish word for the steam that emerges when water is thrown onto the hot sauna stones. Designed by Avanto Architects, the project was commissioned by the city of Helsinki as part of an initiative to develop the former industrial area of Hernesaari into a coastal residential area.

The building's design accommodates for this future growth, including plans to connect the narrow coastal park to a larger, Helsinki-bound parkland. With this in mind, Löyly's elongated design has it perched comfortably on the coastline. The building's shape, too, forms an outdoor auditorium for the local marine sport club's future activities, and its low profile will afford future residential buildings views of the sea beyond. The exterior, a wooden shell of heat-treated pine (Löyly is the first Forest Stewardship Council-certified building in Finland), will blend into the landscape over time, becoming gray like the shoreline rocks. The finely slatted paneling not only creates a Venetian-blind effect from the inside, offering sauna-goers private views to the outdoors, but also shades the interior, reducing future cooling costs for the building, which is powered by water and wind-sourced energy.

Inside, Studio Joanna Laajisto used durable, long-lasting materials including black concrete, blackened steel, wool, and Scandinavian birch wood to construct the three saunas, restaurant, and connecting resting areas. The wood itself is the result of a sustainable Finnish innovation that repurposes leftover materials from the plywood industry. Outside, as is local custom, visitors can swim in the sea and in winter there is a dedicated space for an ice hole (known in Finnish as an *avanto*) to plunge into. Löyly's future-proofed design is not limited to the structure alone, but extends to the culture of Finnish public bathing itself, providing a space for mixed saunas with bathing suits. "Traditionally men and women bathe separately and naked. We wanted to develop sauna culture so that there would be a possibility to bathe together with your friends regardless of gender," shares Avanto of its mindful space. "This makes the sauna experience available also for foreign visitors that might not be used to bathing naked."

ALFA MOVING
PANORAMA
PANORAMA

LÖYLY PUBLIC SAUNA

Löyly Public Sauna is a modern reinterpretation of the communal Finnish bathhouse. Perched on the coast, its exterior pine shell acts as decking (below), inviting outdoor social activity (previous page) in the balmier months. The finely slatted paneling has manifold benefits, letting in daylight, while offering sauna-goers privacy and views to the outdoors (opposite).

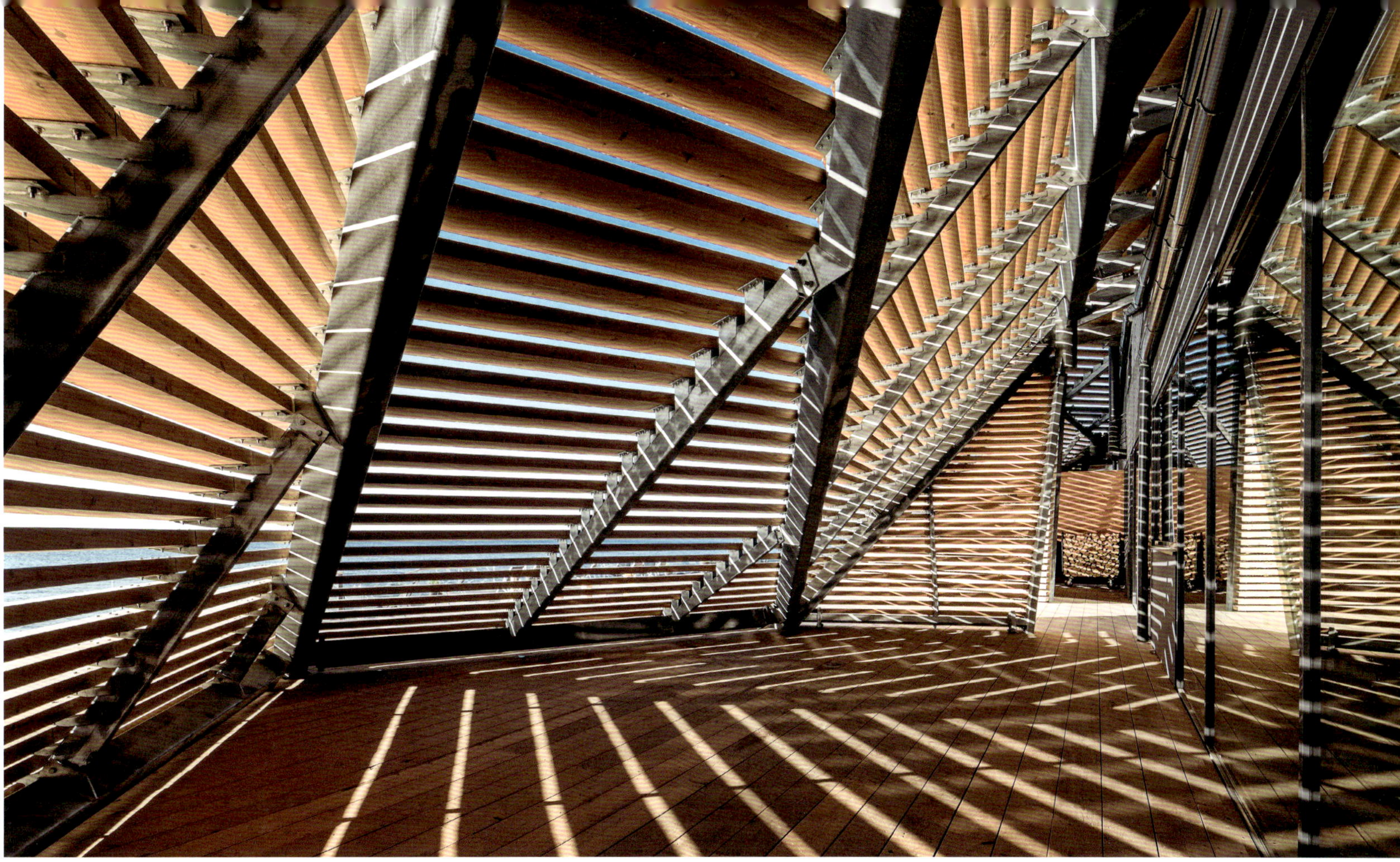

FRANCIS KÉRÉ: A TRUE PROBLEM SOLVER

The Burkinabé, Pritzker Prize winner's people-centric approach enables communities in the Global South to tackle issues of climate and scarcity

In 2022, Diébédo Francis Kéré made history by becoming the first African and the first Black architect to win the Pritzker Architecture Prize, the discipline's most prestigious, since its inception in 1979. Kéré, driven by a deep commitment to community-based architecture as a social good, couldn't be more different from the Pritzker's first laureate, establishment architect par excellence Philip Johnson. Kéré's win suggests the extent to which the architecture world has changed in that time, becoming more closely aligned with the values of architects like himself who are committed to enabling communities from the Global South to solve problems connected to climate change, scarcity, and long-term energy use.

On hearing the news, Kéré recounts that his first thought was disbelief, followed by happiness, and then a sense of responsibility. The prize is accompanied by a substantial financial gift as well as increased media attention—from both the architectural press and mainstream news. For Kéré, the expanded platform provides an opportunity to raise certain issues, not least the importance of

Startup Lions Campus (previous page) employs local quarry stone and stacked towers for passive cooling. The TUM Tower (above), a civic center for the Technical University of Munich, explores the possibilities of geometry, starting from a simple square. The Burkina Faso National Assembly (opposite) is a stepped pyramidal design that foregrounds new views, both literally and figuratively. Its latticed form symbolizes a new transparency between parliament and the people.

representation in a profession notorious for its lack of diversity. "We live in a world that is not in balance when it comes to diversity in most professions," he explains. "Architecture is no different and ... representation is important as it might just give someone who does not see themselves reflected the strength to hang in there when it gets tough. But there is also the need for questioning beyond representation: why it is that you already need certain privileges in order to be able to survive as an architect?"

Born in Gando, a village in land-locked Burkina Faso, West Africa, Kéré understands better than most the tenacity and persistence required to be able to succeed in architecture. Aged seven, he left his village and immediate family to attend school. Six years later, he moved to the east of the country to further his studies, eventually specializing in carpentry. At 17, he received a scholarship from BMZ Deutschland to become a woodwork development activist, arriving in Berlin in 1985. "Leaving home and dealing with the emotions that come with that is something I learned very early," Kéré says. "But leaving was also always connected with a sense that I was doing something for my place of origin."

When Kéré finally embarked on formal architectural education at the Technical University of Berlin in 1995, aged 30, thoughts of "doing something" for Gando were preeminent in his mind. Once enrolled, Kéré's architecture professors encouraged him to pursue his dreams of changing the way buildings are made in Burkina Faso. "What they made me understand is that the way I wanted to build was not just a private pursuit ... but that it could be an important contribution to the field of architecture in general."

In his second year, Kéré began work on a project that would transform architecture in Gando and give something back to his home village. The project was the Gando Primary School, which won Kéré an Aga Khan Award in 2004. Funded by setting up an associated foundation in order to raise money, Kéré realized the project with the collaboration and participation of the community in Gando. The architect has repeatedly stressed the importance of community collaboration in projects such as Gando Primary School; communities have been integral for construction, as well as for maintenance and after-construction care. "People and the world we live in are the start and end point of my work. If there is no one who needs a building then why would I build one?"

he says. "And if no one uses what I have built, then what is the use? A space is only fully realized once it is used."

To this end, Kéré emphasizes the value of providing communities with knowledge rather than mere buildings. Partly, this comes down to his understanding that, in order for his architecture to be impactful, it must be both widespread and adaptable. Given the small size of his studio, there are, of course, only so many buildings that Kéré and his team can design. Realizing this, Kéré says that "people are most empowered when they learn to help themselves and can only truly be free to express themselves and be original in thought if they are not somehow indebted to someone else." Kéré stresses that this is not an ideal grounded in the individual, and acknowledges that humans are social creatures: "But community structures should [have their own knowledge] without an outside entity or an individual professional being able to solely decide their fate." It is this philosophy, as much as his intelligent designs and inspired use of local materials, that has brought Kéré widespread acclaim and recognition.

Though the schools and community projects in Burkina Faso are the heart of Kéré's studio, he is very much in demand beyond the country having completed the Obama Legacy Campus and Startup Lions Campus, both in Kenya, the Benga Riverside Residential Community in Mozambique

For the Burkina Institute of Technology (above), Kéré employed a clay and cement mixture that could be cast on-site and used like traditional concrete. This provides a more thermally protective alternative to stacked bricks that speeds up the construction process while reducing costs. Kéré's 2017 Serpentine Pavilion (opposite), with its eliptical wooden canopy on space-frame legs, is encircled by a dark-blue wall. It mirrors the form of a tree, inviting visitors to gather beneath its shade.

and, more recently, a glass tower inspired by spring maypoles for the Technical University in Munich.
In seeming contrast to his materially driven, small-scale community projects rooted in "an architecture of marginal transformations," Kéré has also designed a number of representational buildings on vast scales. For example, the Benin National Assembly, designed to resemble a palaver tree, a traditional meeting place for debate, or Burkina Faso's pyramid-like National Assembly. Kéré has described these projects as visionary ideas which make a marked impact on the imagination, regardless of whether or not they are ever actually built. At present, they remain in the design phase.

Of his interest in both scales and types of design work, Kéré remarks that, although we think of constraint and freedom as opposites, they can in fact nurture each other if kept in balance. "But you have to know how to do that," he says. "If you focus on what you cannot do when there is scarcity, you limit your freedom of thought and when you leave out even the most practical of constraints, like the need for an opening to enter a building, then the utopian idea is only a philosophical experiment. I like to do architecture that does both. Everyday architecture can be surprising and forward-thinking in minor, but significant, details that can feed the imagination and utopian fantasies can offer solutions for the way we build every day."

With a design team in Berlin and another group of well-trained construction experts in Burkina Faso, Kéré has so far kept his studio small. He likes to work directly with everyone in his team, he says. Whether or not Kéré will be able to maintain such a small studio as demand for his work inevitably increases remains to be seen. More certain is that Kéré's successes point to a profession increasingly receptive to the architect's pressing concerns of material scarcity, climate conditions, and community engagement—an encouraging sign for the future of architecture and of the planet.

"People and the world we live in are the start and end point of my work. If there is no one who needs a building then why would I build one?"

The Center for Health and Social Advancement (above and opposite, top) in Laongo, Burkina Faso is defined by its myriad windows. These offer patients varied views of the landscape beyond its walls, which are made from hollow concrete bricks, covered with clay. The Sarbalé Ke Pavilion (opposite, bottom), made for the 2019 edition of Coachella Festival in California, is an installation of 12 colorful towers inspired by the baobab tree, a community landmark in West Africa.

THE CAMPUS BUILT TO UPLIFT A REGION

STARTUP LIONS CAMPUS
KÉRÉ ARCHITECTURE
TURKANA COUNTY, KENYA

Located on the banks of Lake Turkana, Kenya, the Startup Lions Campus provides vocational opportunities for local youth in a building that is itself designed to thrive. The campus, designed by Kéré Architecture, offers free high-level training in information and communication technologies and is part of a larger initiative to invigorate remote communities by alleviating youth unemployment and preventing local "brain drain."

The campus's form, made up of five interlinked two-story buildings, references a natural phenomenon common in the region: the towering mound networks built by termite colonies. "The project celebrates the unique morphology and natural beauty of its site," say the architects. The inspiration is beyond aesthetic and employs nature's tried and tested expertise in surviving the Kenyan heat. The result is a sustainable structure that is uniquely heat resilient. Using the so-called "stack effect," tall ventilation towers jut upwards from the low-lying buildings, naturally cooling the working areas by ferrying warm air upwards while fresh air circulates inside through low-level openings with woven-straw shades. These also serve to protect the IT equipment from corrosive dust. The buildings are topped with terraces tumbling with creeping plants that offer a wondrous setting for ideation and informal meetings with views over Lake Turkana.

The materials, too, are of thoughtful local origin. "In choosing which materials and construction techniques to use, ecological sustainability, cost, and availability factors were weighed to arrive at the best compromise," explain the architects, who involved locals in the design, decision-making, and construction process to create a building that could truly serve the community. The campus is built of low-cost, locally sourced quarry stone finished with a terracotta-colored plaster. Executed by local craftsmen, the chosen hue allows the structure to blend into the landscape as seamlessly as a termite mound.

A HOMAGE TO PLACE AND PEOPLE

PIROUETTE HOUSE

WALLMAKERS

THIRUVANANTHAPURAM, INDIA

Pirouette House in Thiruvananthapuram, in India's Kerala, is a tribute to its locality, championing the area's dwindling brick-making tradition, employing vernacular materials, and minimizing waste. The urban home was designed by sustainability-focused architects Wallmakers, and pays homage to the late British-born Indian architect Laurie Baker, a Thiruvananthapuram resident, who pioneered the use of local materials to create eco-friendly buildings.

The building was built using "rat trap bond" masonry, introduced by Baker in Kerala, where bricks are laid vertically to create strong, hollow walls. The cost-effective technique usefully conceals structural elements and service ducts, reducing energy consumption via passive cooling. From here, the building's undulating facade was born. "The idea was developed to form a series of slanting walls that danced left and right, converging to support the ferro-cement shell roof. Each staggered wall has been tailor-made to suit the issue of deficiency in space that this residence posed, aiming to create larger volumes and a feeling of privacy," explains Wallmakers. The building houses a kitchen, living-dining room, and bedroom on the ground floor, and two further bedrooms, bathrooms, and an informal living area upstairs.

The house respects its environment by using vernacular and upcycled materials. A clever use of thin, steel-reinforced arched shells (called MMT Ferrocement shells), lowered cement consumption by 40 percent and the use of steel by 30 percent. The remaining materials are derived from the build and the region: scaffolding pipes from the construction form the staircase and grillwork, and leftover planks were pieced together to form part of the flooring. Local cane from the neighborhood was treated and used to create subtle privacy screens and pieces of bespoke furniture, while the structure's walls were finished in earthy, local oxides, at once resourceful and a visual expression of Kerala.

Pirouette House celebrates Kerala's brick-making tradition, using the locally pioneered, eco-friendly "rat trap bond" masonry method (previous page) to create a passively cooled house. The supporting curved walls minimize the overall materials, creating an efficient external structure. Meanwhile, on the inside, the staircase is upcycled from the construction site's scaffolding, while local woven cane was employed to create privacy screens (above).

A BAMBOO PAVILION ON THE FRINGE OF NATURE

VEDANA RESTAURANT
VTN ARCHITECTS
NINH BÌNH, VIETNAM

The Vedana Restaurant is a lakeside bamboo structure that frames the landscape at the foothills of Cuc Phuong's rolling rainforest mountains. Designed by VTN Architects, the building, an all-day restaurant and event space, is at the heart of the Vedana Resort, on the fringe of north Vietnam's Cuc Phuong National Park, the country's oldest nature reserve.

The large structure spans 1,050 m² (11,302 ft²) and is made entirely of local bamboo to reflect the region's architecture. The striking, three-gabled thatched roof is made of two stacked ring-shaped roofs topped with a dome. Each layer is connected by an inward-slanting row of thin bamboo strips that, in addition to structural support, allows light and ventilation. "The stepped roof, inspired by traditional architecture, is made of 36 modular frames that appear like a multi-level structure, yet they are on a single floor," explain the architects. With the largest radius, measuring 18 m (59 ft), and with the building's height of 16 m (52 ft), it is the tallest bamboo structure designed by the Vietnamese studio to date.

The restaurant was strategically placed on the bank of a lake, which functions as a natural air-conditioner. "Making use of the lake is essential concerning the hot and humid weather during the summer in Cuc Phuong Commune in particular and northern Vietnam in general," the architects explain. Inside the cavernous building, guests can marvel at the complexity of the bamboo structure and its interior arches, and find relief from the heat while enjoying views and outdoor access. To provide further wonder, the lake irrigates the resort's plant life, including the 15,000 recently planted blossom trees that will one day surround the restaurant. From inside the building, visitors will always be connected to Cuc Phuong, say the architects. "The view towards the blossoming forest, the mountains, and the lake are omnipresent for visitors even from the middle of the dome-shaped structure."

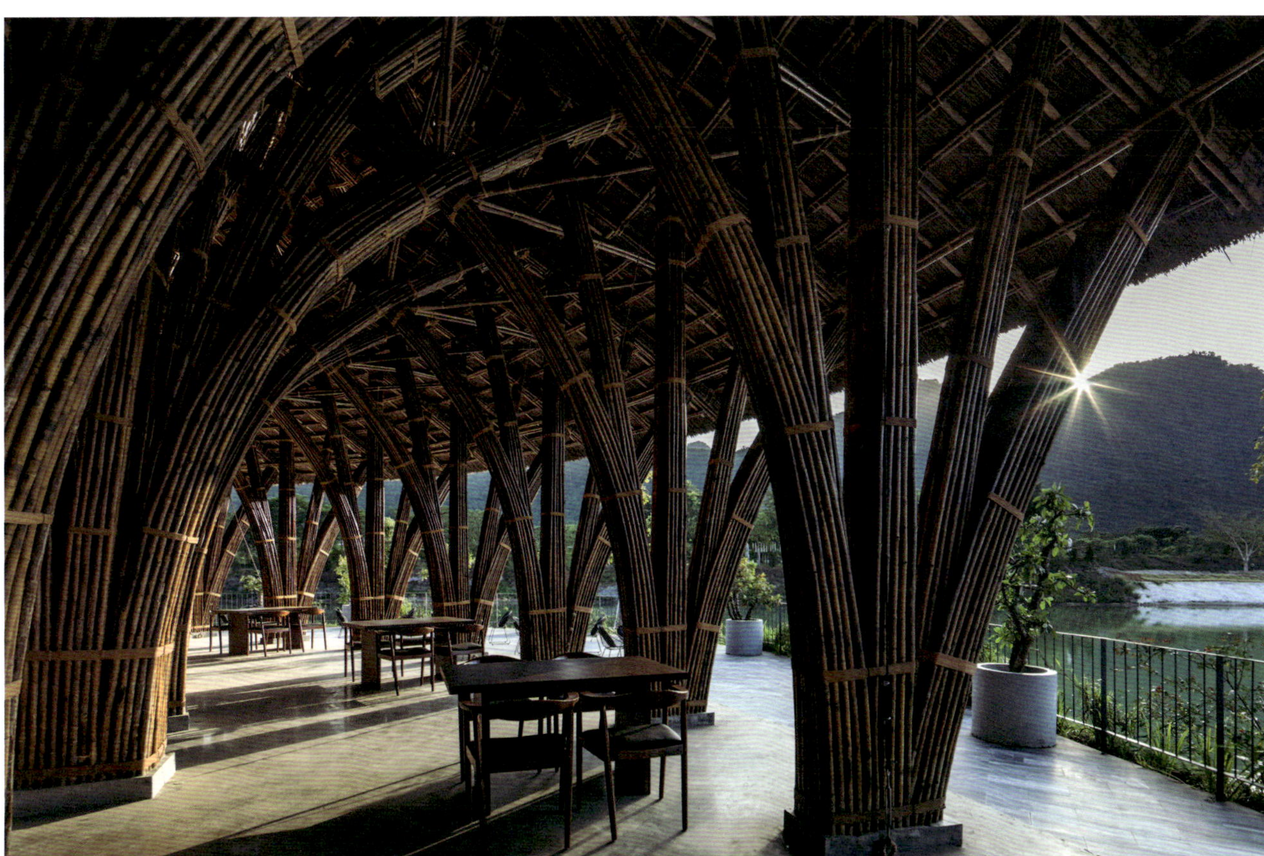

VEDANA RESTAURANT

The Vedana Restaurant is a cavernous, bamboo structure that overlooks a lake at the foot of Cuc Phuong National Park's mountains. The stepped roof (previous page and opposite, top) is inspired by local architecture and appears patterned from the inside, guiding diners' gazes upwards (above). The shaded interior provides relief from the tropical heat, catching the refreshing breeze that comes off the lake.

A DIGNIFIED HOME FOR A RECYCLING INITIATIVE

LA COMUNA

NATURA FUTURA ARQUITECTURA + FRONTERA SUR ARQUITECTURA

HUAQUILLAS, ECUADOR

La Comuna (meaning the municipality or commune) is a structure that gives back to the community twofold, providing space to facilitate different kinds of recycling, and a home for the family dedicating themselves to this vital local initiative. The vernacular structure, located in Huaquillas, a southern Ecuadorian town on the Peruvian border, was commissioned by a private enterprise to help the family, who were previously living and processing local recycling in a shack. The striking new structure not only provides them with dignified living quarters and a space better suited to their important environmental work, but it also establishes a prominent public profile for their efforts. "As a production space, La Comuna seeks to maintain a constant dialogue with the development of the city through the different activities that are developed inside and outside the proposal, generating an intermediary to facilitate a productive process chain and promote the entrepreneurship of the users," explain architects Natura Futura Arquitectura and Frontera Sur Arquitectura.

The two-level structure is made of wood, in tune with the surrounding local buildings, with shafts and latticework bringing in ventilated and controlled light to suit the tropical climate. The upstairs and downstairs are divided between workshop and home, with various modular elements allowing for flexible use of the space. "The house starts from the contrast between experiment and project, proposing intervention strategies with spatial permeability and self-management of space." Each floor is made up of three modules. Downstairs, there is a designated zone for recycling, with the waste differentiated in each room according to material. Upstairs are the family's modular private living areas, arranged in three 12 m² (129 ft²) rooms. On hand are dividing partitions fitted with wheels so that the family can arrange their space as they wish.

The layout of the building, with its open, ground-floor processing site, invites the community to engage with recycling. Even the upper facade bears a message, with the imperative slogan "RECICLA" (recycle), cut into the latticework. As the architects explain: "La Comuna [is] a milestone for the city, due to the transformation process it had, with a history of unhealthiness and contamination. The project communicates a discourse through its facade with a message, generating reflection between the private and the public through architecture and recycling."

La Comuna is both a home and a headquarters for the recycling movement in southern Ecuador. The lattice-work on the wooden facade (page 190) is punctuated with the catchy call to *recicla* (recycle). Downstairs houses the open-to-the-public waste differentiation center (opposite and below), while upstairs functions as the family's private living quarters (page 191).

Identity: A Result, Not a Starting Point

A renewed appreciation for vernacular building methods and materials is shaping new architecture across the globe—vitally reinforcing local identity

When the jury picked Burkinabé architect Francis Kéré as the 2022 Pritzker Prize laureate, they were simultaneously celebrating an emerging form of architectural practice now found across the world—the adaptation of local, traditional construction techniques as an effective response to resource shortages, local conditions, and, by extension, the climate crisis. This is something that Kéré has mastered, while simultaneously harnessing the aesthetic impact of such techniques and materials to help forge a sense of identity, one that links the past with the present to conjure a distinct and important sense of place.

As poorer nations often do not possess the political influence or media power of their wealthier counterparts, their cultures are frequently dominated by richer nations at the expense of their own. As Kéré once said: "The West knows how to present its culture. Everybody is dominated by the images produced in the West."[1] This supremacy affects the discourse and imagery surrounding different societies' progress and economic development and, by extension, the planning and design processes of their cities. Kéré understands this and has deliberately set out to challenge it, providing cheap and climate-appropriate solutions that both involve and represent the communities they are designed for.

Ecuador's Provider Productive Center (above) uses local handmade bricks.

And he is not the only proponent of such ideas. In certain disadvantaged areas in Latin America,[2] a scarcity of resources and the absence of the state have provided young architects the scope to step in and create public spaces, giving rise to so-called "social" or "informal"[3] architecture. This has led to the renewed embrace of local technical approaches and aesthetic identities: limited budgets have been offset by the use of local materials; construction and urban-planning solutions have been designed without regulatory cover, and community efforts have been harnessed for the construction process.

Initiatives such as the Taller Social Latinoamericano (TSL, or Latin American Social Workshop), a two-week workshop led by the Coordinadora Latinoamericana de Estudiantes de Arquitectura (Latin American Coordinator of Architecture Students), have been pivotal in such endeavors. Since 2004, TSL has brought together architecture students and emerging architecture firms—such as Ruta 4 Taller (Colombia), Entre Nos Atelier (Costa Rica), Rama Estudio (Ecuador), and Taller de Diseño Cooperativo (Argentina)—to analyze, design, and build public spaces on the outskirts of cities situated everywhere from Mexico to Peru. Central to TSL's projects is the creation of architecture that establishes a sense of identity to empower and uplift communities who would most likely otherwise be overlooked by formal design experts and planners.

Ruta 4 Taller's Community Sewing Workshop Amairis in San Isidro, Colombia, is an example of one such building: a cutting and sewing factory run by members of the village community that employs materials (namely Colombian timber bamboo and brick and clay tiles) and techniques local to the region to holistic and innovative effect. Both symbolically and literally, the resulting building, installed with clever yet simple devices that manage the impact of the hot climate, stands as a testament to the skilled craftsmanship the community has fostered.

In Ecuador, the financial crisis of 1999 spawned a whole generation of contemporary architects, influenced by Spanish architect José María Sáez, championing a bold,

La Pradería updates local architecture methods to facilitate the playing of indoor sports. Its folding metal panels promote better ventilation (above, top).

La Pradería Sports Integration Center for Rural Areas, Ecuador (above).

new "do more with less" approach. This figure of speech, coined by Ana María Durán Calisto,[4] is the subject of Chilean/Spanish director duo Kliwadenko Novas' 2017 documentary of the same name. Indeed, *Do More With Less* is an excellent study of the ways in which materiality in modern Ecuadorian architecture exists hand-in-hand with identity and sustainability. Among other projects, it spotlights the coastal Escuela Nueva Esperanza (New Hope School) by Al Borde—a playful, boat-shaped learning space made from local, low-impact materials including timber, bamboo, and knitted straw scarf. In an area where most schools are rendered in bleak gray concrete and drop-out levels are high, this natural beacon of hope fosters unity, identity, and pride.

In Babahoyo and Montalvo, meanwhile, Ecuadorian architecture firm Natura Futura has been busy reviving and reinventing the use of brick as well as local building methods. In small Ecuadorian towns such as these, the tendency is to imitate the trends of nearby Guayaquil, where building in concrete, in this instance, is a common status symbol, despite its thermal inefficiency in humid climates. In response to this, the studio designed a simple but elegant structure for the Centro Rural de Integración Deportiva La Pradería (La Pradería Sports Integration Center for Rural Areas), reinterpreting local architecture to facilitate sport activities. Supported by two brick walls, the building's two-story facade consists of folding metal panels made of wooden lattice and mosquito screening that provides ventilation and protection for players, while offering an inventive modern take on the area's traditional masonry techniques.

It is important to note, however, that identities are, of course, changeable and very much related to a country's urban, social, environmental, and cultural context. Thus, some of the most successful identity-reinforcing architectural projects are the ones that can be shaped by, and adapted to, their shifting surroundings.

Kéré revived traditional materials and building methods for his school in Gando (above, bottom) and his facilities for Mali's National Park (above, top).

Kéré's Startup Lions Campus (above) optimizes local Kenyan techniques.

The internationally admired architecture of 1990s Chile, for instance, was marked by its experimental housing design, in both materials and form, framed by the country's breathtaking landscapes and nudged by the cultural boom that followed the end of the military dictatorship in 1990. However, the widespread embrace of this austere aesthetic, defined by its use of raw materials and starkly shaped volumes, would hinder the development of new architectural approaches in the years (and arguably decades[5]) that followed. But of course, Chile has experienced significant changes in the past 30 years, defined by a stronger middle-class agenda and a focus on improved quality of life in cities, requiring an architecture that reflects this. Happily, a number of contemporary architects have risen to this challenge, bringing together old with new to reflect the country's evolving identity.

Indeed, history has played a fundamental role in Chile's most recent contemporary public architecture. Buildings damaged by the 1973–90 military dictatorship, such as La Moneda and the UNCTAD III, have resulted in newly adjacent or refurbished projects that deliberately promote democracy through pedestrian-friendly, indoor public spaces. These are, more often than not, large in scale with a cultural bent. Of particular note is UNCTAD III, which, after the 1973 *coup d'etat*, housed the regime's executive branch for eight years marking a powerful political gesture. A fire in 2006 led to a public design competition for the Gabriela Mistral Cultural Center in the same plot. Incorporating what remained of the building, Cristián Fernández Arquitectos and Lateral Arquitectura & Diseño worked together to reinvigorate and extend the space. This is wrapped in a perforated copper "skin" that simultaneously illustrates and celebrates the value of Chilean copper and symbolizes a new, more transparent relationship between institutions and citizens.

In the case of the Pereira Palace, meanwhile, an eclectic 19th-century mansion that was badly damaged, first by an earthquake and then by careless intervention during the 1970s, clever adaptive reuse on behalf of architects Cecilia Puga, Paula Velasco, and Alberto Moletto has led to the unique preservation of a national heritage site. Exposed bricks reveal the mansion's original masonry, while a new structure in reinforced concrete respectfully unites the palace's original design with a new grid solution. This is delineated by copper-coated bridges and stairs that introduce a compelling contemporary vernacular appropriate for the building's new role as the country's Ministry of Cultures, Arts, and Heritage.

While this essay has only touched upon a few examples of identity-reinforcing architecture, in a purely Latin American context it demonstrates some of the many innovative forms that establishing, enhancing, or even shaping a sense of local or national identity through building can take. Regardless of the budget or the local conditions, the majority succeed in establishing a delicate balance between reformulation and new discourses. They are shaped by real conditions and local materials, by heritage and storied techniques, while simultaneously harnessing contemporary advancements where it makes sense to do so. They speak to, and also for, the people and geography they are designed for. As stated by Kéré, a building is "something that everyone understands and feels proud to be part of,"[6] and, in pursuing identity, these works function uniquely in the place to which they belong.

Some of the most successful identity-reinforcing architectural projects are the ones that can be shaped by, and adapted to, their shifting surroundings.

Daniel Moreno Flores and Sebastián Calero's House in Carrizal, Ecuador (above, both) repurposes local materials from a nearby museum building site.

GOOD ARCHITECTURE IS PROTECTIVE

Protective architecture provides sanctuary through design. It considers what we need sheltering from—both now and in the future, across different scales—and creates spaces accordingly

Architecture as shelter is a concept largely overlooked nowadays, mostly relegated to the realms of social housing, projects for migrants, and victims of natural and human-made disasters. Yet protection permeates every architectural project in some shape or form. Residential skyscrapers in wealthy, densely populated cities are never viewed as simply "shelter for humans." Instead, with help from real-estate marketers and glitzy press releases, they are linked to social status and a luxury lifestyle. But no matter how much they are designed and billed to make their inhabitants feel special, residential skyscrapers—like each and every building we occupy—must first and foremost make people feel safe.

If humans have always sought shelter from weather conditions, wild animals, enemy cities, and natural disasters in their architecture, today a new layer has emerged: everything we thought we knew about what our cities must be prepared for is under scrutiny in our global age of uncertainty and unpredictability.

Global warming and the progressive loss of biodiversity makes for a discouraging forecast that suggests that soon we will all be living in a permanent state of reconstruction. Indeed, future mitigation plans in dense urban zones will be shaped mostly by the climate crisis, and new challenges will likely include the relocation of entire neighborhoods as sea levels increase or the creation of new risk zones in already dense areas as the result of other natural disasters. Tackling such problems will require new solutions.

In order to protect, good architecture should be resilient, but true resilience must take many forms—beyond demonstrating mere material strength—as revealed when it is put to the test. As Professor Cem Kayatekin notes, when it comes to architecture's "infrastructure, institutional networks, energy and waste systems, and carbon footprints, we must assume the material science definition of resilience, [while in] the realm of the socio-economic, the political, and the cultural we must assume the ecological definition of resilience." In other words, just as jungles retain a broad enough diversity and range of scales to survive such catastrophes as droughts or fires, cities can be strengthened by incorporating a variety of architectural typologies and scales, or by approaching the notion of protection in multiple ways.

This might involve reviving time-honored vernacular techniques and materials in extreme climates, and pairing them with new technologies where relevant to optimize their efficiency. Or, on an entirely local scale, it may also require designing a protective shelter based on traditional rural hay sheds to create a safe haven in the harsh environs of the Australian outback.

Some of the best examples of protective architecture, meanwhile, not only serve humans, but nurture wildlife and nature also. Take, for instance, the various shelters for rehabilitating endangered species that are springing up in some of the world's most sensitive and biodiverse nature reserves. This kind of typology provides an exclusive opportunity to serve a second purpose: to increase wildlife protection awareness among visitors and the local community, teaching them to value, respect, and nourish the ecosystem that surrounds them.

Architects, urban planners, designers, policymakers, and citizens face a common challenge: how to imagine, plan, design, build, and maintain an architecture that mirrors and understands uncertainty, and the need for flexibility in order to truly protect those that inhabit it.

We know how modernism flagged the key preoccupations of the last century in the cities it created and fostered: industrialization, optimization, and rationalization underscored every layer of the built environment to great effect, until humanity's preoccupations changed direction rendering such modes of building outdated. Today, there is more need than ever before to protect ourselves and our planet, both now and for the future, and the projects included in this chapter signal some of the most effective architectural solutions currently being put forward in order to do so across various scales and typologies.

A MONUMENT TO A RESTORED ECOSYSTEM

WASIT NATURAL RESERVE VISITOR CENTER

X ARCHITECTS

SHARJAH, UNITED ARAB EMIRATES

The Wasit Natural Reserve Visitor Center in Sharjah, United Arab Emirates, is a tribute to the site's revival from environmental collapse. In the 1970s and 1980s, during the rapid urbanization of the city, Sharjah's coastal wetlands and salt marshes became a waste-water and rubbish dump. But in 2005, a huge environmental initiative began to restore the damaged ecosystem. As part of the clean up, 40,000 m² (430,556 ft²) of rubbish was removed and 35,000 trees were re-planted. Today, the land is considered the green lung of Sharjah, and is again made up of wetlands, unique salt flats, and coastal sand dunes. It is once more home to 350 species of non-migratory birds and is a landing zone for 33,000 migrating birds.

Designed by X Architects, the visitor center encourages the continued preservation of the site environment by educating visitors on the surrounding ecosystem and its avian species. The low-lying building is accessed through a sloping ramp that guides visitors into three different axes: a space for services and administrative offices; a cafe and multipurpose space with views of the wetlands; and, in-between, a long viewing gallery with a cantilevered roof that allows uninterrupted views, through floor-to-ceiling glass, of six canopied aviaries. Though formally similar, each of these has been designed—in collaboration with biologists and zoologists—to foster different wetland microclimates for the area's key bird species. Made from recycled wood and plastic materials used on-site, as well as tailored netting solutions, every aviary boasts its own array of plants, trees, landscaping techniques, and climate-control systems. By physically dividing the spaces, the spread of disease between habitats is prevented.

As a whole, the visitor center takes advantage of "the site's natural topography to minimize its visual impact by making it appear submerged into the ground," the architects explain. The interior, too, is starkly minimalistic and limited to the informative displays on the supporting central wall. On the outside, the tilted, glazed facade has a dual benefit, and is angled slightly to enhance reflections of the landscape of the birds, while minimizing reflections inside for birdwatchers, who can sit on the concrete bench along the perimeter of the sunken gallery to observe the birds at their level. To further give back to the site, rainwater harvested on the insulated roof is directed to specific areas of the landscape by way of camouflaged irrigation.

WASIT NATURAL RESERVE
VISITOR CENTER

The UAE's Wasit Natural Reserve Visitor Center has revived a damaged ecosystem into a flourishing natural reserve complete with a visitor center (previous page). The viewing gallery allows visitors to observe the canopied aviaries (above and opposite, top) that act as microclimates for the local species, while the overall profile of the center is kept low so as to minimally interrupt the setting (opposite, bottom).

طيور البحيرات
Lagoon Birds

A HOUSE THAT GIVES BACK

CASA MARTHA

NASO

OCUILAN, MEXICO

Casa Martha is an accessible home built as part of a charitable initiative to house and uplift a Mexican community badly affected by a series of earthquakes in 2017. So far, the charity, ReConstruir México (Reconstruct Mexico), has realized 16 sustainable homes in Oculian, Mexico State.

Architects Naso approached the design by ascertaining the exact needs of the residents, two elderly parents and their two adult children. A truly accessible design became their focal point: the elderly mother had mobility issues, while the father suffered from blindness. Around this, three ideas emerged. According to Naso, these included: "Firstly, to generate efficient and clear circulations within the house to ensure the parents could be as independent as possible. Secondly, to promote the coexistence between parents and children, as well as respecting their privacy. Finally, to include spaces that could open possibilities and potentially facilitate the chance of additional income for the family."

Built from compacted earth blocks manufactured on site, the structure is made up of a rectangular ground floor and a semi-detached upper level shaped like an arched tower. The ground level houses the kitchen and dining room, as well as a bathroom and two bedrooms. The main bedroom, intended for the parents and built with accessibility in mind, is level with the kitchen and dining area, and its doorway aligns exactly with the bathroom to provide a clear access route. As the house is located between an archaeological site and one of Mexico's most important pilgrimage sites, a clever economic offering was built into the plans. The third bedroom is located in the semi-detached part of the building accessed via an outdoor staircase and contains its own roof terrace, giving greater privacy to the occupant. It was intended to be used by one of the children, but may be rented out as lodgings for tourists in this area, providing the family with a source of income.

Casa Martha is an accessible home built for an elderly Mexican couple and their adult son. The thoughtful, ground-level layout allows the couple to easily navigate, and enjoy, their living space, with direct connection to the outdoors (above). While the vaulted tower (page 205) and rooftop terrace (opposite, top) act as a separate wing for the son or rentable accommodation to provide added income.

A MINIMALIST TAKE ON THE AUSTRALIAN HAYSHED

SHACK IN THE ROCKS
SEAN GODSELL ARCHITECTS
VICTORIA, AUSTRALIA

Shack in the Rocks is a streamlined reinterpretation of the Australian hayshed. The Shack is located approximately one hour's drive west of Melbourne just behind some protected granite ridges called the You Yangs. The exposed plot is characterized by the presence of granite boulders, giving the Shack its name. Here, Sean Godsell Architects have created an arcadian, cost-effective house for weekend retreats.

The architects began considering the environmental requirements. "We noted the primary requirement in rural and outback Australia for shelter: a roof parasol that provides some shade and protection from the rain as well as a place to enjoy outdoor activities—cooking, eating, and engaging with and framing the site's spectacular landscape," they explain.

The hayshed, ubiquitous in rural Australia, is referenced in the flat, steel-roof structure and utilitarian, living spaces. "We modified this by including a translucent roofing material for light and adapting some industrial walkway grating to make a louver for shade," say the architects. "Within the 100 m² (1,076 ft²) planned space, only 30 m² (323 ft²) is accommodation space, divided between two pods. Two translucent 'sheds' are positioned to the east end of a monolithic concrete plinth: one shed for cooking and eating and the other for sleeping and ablutions."

The atypical hierarchy was inspired by Japanese architect Riken Yamamoto's creative deconstruction of residential layouts, also arranged across a single platform. "This highly poetic scattering of spaces is controlled by a large shallow gable roof that shelters not only the rooms but the outdoor or 'other' space in the building," explains Godsell of the reference. In the case of the Shack, the arrangement merges modest indoor and outdoor spaces under one protective shelter, encouraging a restoratively minimalist getaway in easy communion with its setting.

LIQUID HISTORY HOUSED IN MODERN BARNS

KYRÖ DISTILLERY COMPANY BARREL STORAGE

AVANTO ARCHITECTS

ISOKYRÖ, FINLAND

The Kyrö Distillery Company, in the village of Isokyrö, Finland, uses a barn-inspired approach to house the precise art of whiskey distillation. The craft spirits company is the world's northernmost gin and whiskey producer, and has received numerous accolades in its short history. To aid expansion, Kyrö launched a design competition that was won, and taken on, by the Finnish architects Avanto.

Right from the beginning, the structural design was influenced by the ecological and cultural significance of the site's forest setting. "The area is unique," the architects say of the location, also home to flying squirrels. "The Kyrö river area is classified as a nationally important landscape, with well-preserved farmhouses and vast, flat fields with old wooden barns. This gave us the idea to design the storage buildings as traditional barns, clad in wooden planks, and hiding in the middle of the forest," they say.

Safety then dictated the layout: the design was required to conform to the strict regulations that govern the storage of whiskey, a classified-flammable liquid. "This is why the space needed to be divided into five separate compartments," the designers explain. "Each room has a strictly controlled indoor climate with certain temperature and humidity [settings]. The amount of alcohol evaporating from the wooden barrels is measured so that the air doesn't become flammable."

Although closely resembling the local wooden barns that inspired their exterior, the five spacious structures that make up the project are not, in fact, made of timber. Instead, a risk-averse approach was taken to effectively house the precarious business of whiskey distillation. "In order to call spirit 'whiskey,' you need to store it for at least three years in wooden barrels. Huge storage buildings need to be constructed even if you don't know whether the product will sell well after the storage period," explain the architects. "To minimize risks, the buildings were assembled from standard concrete pillars, beams, and elements, unlike in the first sketches that were based on wooden structures." The distillery's exterior is made of concrete, cast in a mold made of wooden planks taken from a dismantled barn that belonged to the mother-in-law of one of the distillery owners, they add. "Funnily, concrete reproduces the weathered-wood material so well that many people have been touching the facade and still believing it is wood," the designers remark of the functional and unexpectedly whimsical structures.

SCULPTURAL SECLUSION IN URBAN CASABLANCA

VILLA Z

MOHAMED AMINE SIANA

CASABLANCA, MOROCCO

Despite overlooking a busy Casablanca avenue, Villa Z's sculptural design shields it from the bustling city, providing a calm, light-flooded retreat. Architect Mohamed Amine Siana's design cleverly embeds a contemporary home within urban Casablanca by referencing the city's modernist buildings while remaining sensitive to tradition. "The project draws its inspiration from Moroccan cultural roots, while opening up to new horizons," says Siana. "In the city of Casablanca, traditional modernism has been the norm in recent years. It was a laboratory for some brilliant architects and this villa does well to not poke anyone in the eye while in the same breath maintaining a characteristic, distinct plausibility to its integrity as a modern artifact in the city."

Given a small block to work with, and strict city planning regulations, Siana worked outward from the structural blueprint of the cube, subverting it with curvatures. "My principal intention was to go out from this cuboid perception to answer to the client's program and routine, and to find the best way to preserve privacy and protect the project from the noise of the prominent front avenue," explains the architect. "The intention was—working closely with the client's lifestyle in mind—to build a house with discretion and introversion. The design centers on the opacity of the main facade, combining the principles of traditional architecture with a strong contemporary identity." Following the program, the west-facing facade is devoid of any visible openings to the street. Down a path, the front door is hidden behind elegant wooden paneling while intersecting shapes conceal the windows, angled efficiently towards sun-catching aspects. Large windows on the rear facade overlook a pool and are angled inwards, away from neighbors, flooding the open-plan space with light, with an "automatized" roof canopy that allows for climate control. Using its angular geometry and the fluidity of sculpture, the design provides privacy without compromising open airiness and has the added environmentmental benefit of passive cooling.

With its white facade, angles, and curves, the building addresses the cultural shift underway in Morocco, balancing the contemporary with the local flavor of modernism and the traditional desire for a private home. "The project is an experience in which we try to develop practical spaces for the new way of Moroccan life, a cultural dilemma between privacy and the contemporary, open way of life," explains Siana.

Villa Z creatively seals itself off from its bustling Casablanca location, creating a calm and private family home. The dwelling takes inspiration from the city's unique expression of modernist architecture. Windows and light shafts are hidden from street level within the curved geometry of its shell, while on the inside, the open-plan interior is cleverly drenched with light (opposite, bottom).

A RADICALLY RADIAL, CLIMATE-PROOF SCHOOL

LYCÉE SCHORGE SECONDARY SCHOOL

KÉRÉ ARCHITECTURE

KOUDOUGOU, BURKINA FASO

The Lycée Schorge Secondary School rises to the challenge of Burkina Faso's extreme climate, enveloping students in a building where learning may flourish. The country's dry, tropical climate is prone to extreme drought and flooding. The school is located in Koudougou, Burkina Faso's third most populous city and was designed by Kéré Architecture, known for its Afrofuturist vision and resourcefulness.

The design balances sustainability and cost-effective materials to respond to the environment, providing an inspiring place to learn. The school is made up of nine modules arranged in a radial configuration that houses classrooms, administration rooms, and a dental clinic. The spaces are a masterclass in passive cooling techniques: the structure is built using thermally efficient bricks, made from locally harvested laterite stone, and is set under a shady, overhanging roof fitted with various towers to expel hot air. The classrooms' undulating ceilings, made of plaster and concrete components, further aid ventilation with offset spacing that allows the rooms to "breathe and expel hot stagnant air." The light-hued shade also diffuses the daylight, softening the heat of the scorching sunlight.

The building is encased in a protective "secondary" facade of wooden screens for shade, made from local fast-growing wood. In addition to shielding against corrosive wind and dust, the structure creates an indoor gathering space for students waiting to attend class. Meanwhile the building's radial configuration creates a naturally sheltered outdoor courtyard in the inner ring, ready for school and community use.

"The architecture not only functions as a marker in the landscape, it is also a testament to how local materials, in combination with creativity and teamwork, can be transformed into something significant with profound lasting effects," explain the architects of the school, whose design they hope will inspire further education institutions in the region.

LYCÉE SCHORGE SECONDARY SCHOOL

The Lycée Schorge Secondary School protects students from the harsh climate of Burkina Faso with its radial design. On the inside, it creates a wind-proofed courtyard (page 217) for the greater community. The outer ring of classrooms are kept cool with overhanging roofs and towers (page 216) to expel hot air and are connected via a series of shaded indoor-outdoor passageways (opposite, top).

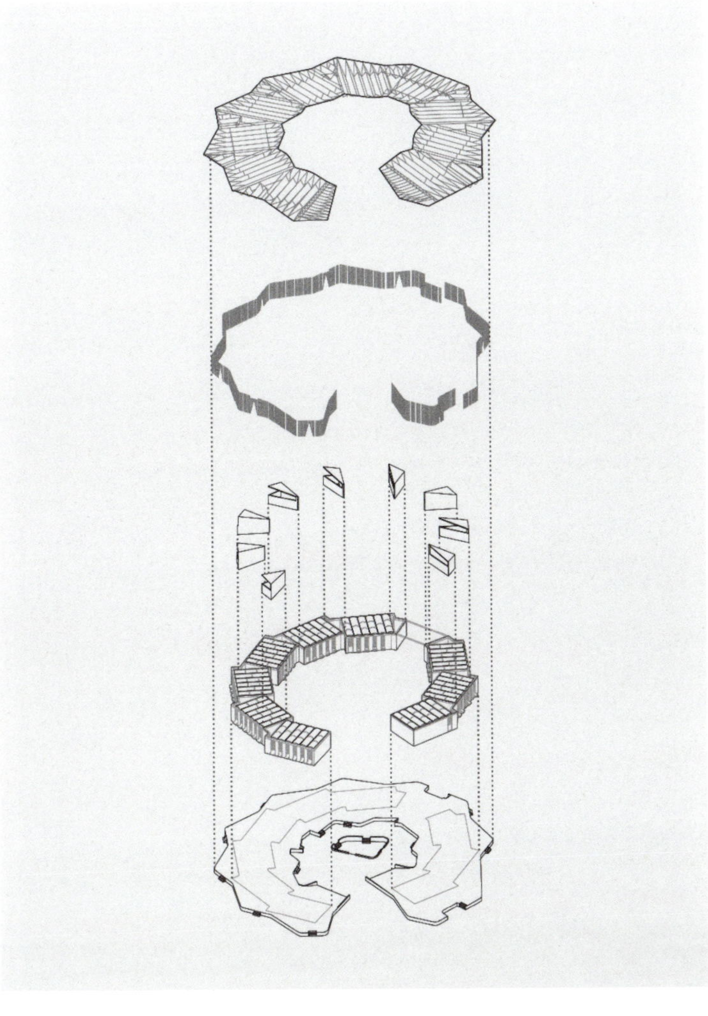

WHERE TURTLES, BIRDS, AND KNOWLEDGE FLOURISH

KHOR KALBA TURTLE AND WILDLIFE SANCTUARY

HOPKINS ARCHITECTS

SHARJAH, UNITED ARAB EMIRATES

Set in one of the United Arab Emirates' most biodiverse nature reserves, the Khor Kalba Turtle and Wildlife Sanctuary champions both public environmental awareness and dedicated conservation. Commissioned by the Environmental Protected Areas Authority in Sharjah and designed by Hopkins Architects, the sanctuary is set on the shores of Khor Kalba, a tidal estuary that trickles into the Gulf of Oman. It is home to one of the most northerly mangrove forests in the world and its unique, attendant wildlife.

The sanctuary features a cluster of seven interlinked pods that function as the visitor center, encouraging the public to learn about the coastal ecosystem and engage with conservation programs. The buildings house aquaria, exhibition areas, visitor amenities, staff offices, and classrooms, as well as a gift shop and cafe. The pods are interlinked and offer panoramic views of the sanctuary through a generous terrace and wide windows. Adjacent to the visitor center is an on-site wildlife care facility, where rescued birds, turtles, and other animals can be tended to, as well as a scientific research base for the reserve and the broader east coast of the United Arab Emirates and Oman. Already, the biodiversity project has seen 1,000 species recorded in the area.

The cluster of buildings creates a sanctuary for rehabilitated turtles, who gather in the dedicated turtle pool, a watering hole that draws in local birdlife too. The sanctuary's outdoor design also contains an aviary dedicated to endangered birds, a mangrove boardwalk, and bird hides. "A carefully set out nature trail encourages visitors to explore the reserve's rich biodiversity of indigenous mangrove forests and mudflats and the species it supports including turtles, stingrays, gazelles, and the rare Arabian Collared Kingfisher," Hopkins Architects explains.

To minimize the sanctuary's footprint—structurally, environmentally, and visually—the build was guided by the principles of passive design. The pods, inspired by urchin exo-skeltons, are made of precast-concrete shells set on disk-like concrete foundations that have minimal impact on the terrain. The well-sealed structures are thermally robust and completely insulated to minimize future energy consumption. To protect against the harsh coastal climate, the buildings are raised, sealed by a waterproof membrane in the cladding, and supported by steel ribs that hug the pale ribbed exteriors, made to reference the nearby shells washing up on the sand.

KHOR KALBA TURTLE AND WILDLIFE SANCTUARY

The Khor Kalba Turtle and Wildlife Sanctuary brings public attention in the UAE to the vital work of conservation. The site is made up of a cluster of buildings (above) that have minimal impact on the terrain and encircle a pond for the rehabilitating turtles (previous page, top). A nature trail enables exploration of the surrounding mudflats and mangroves and their flora and fauna.

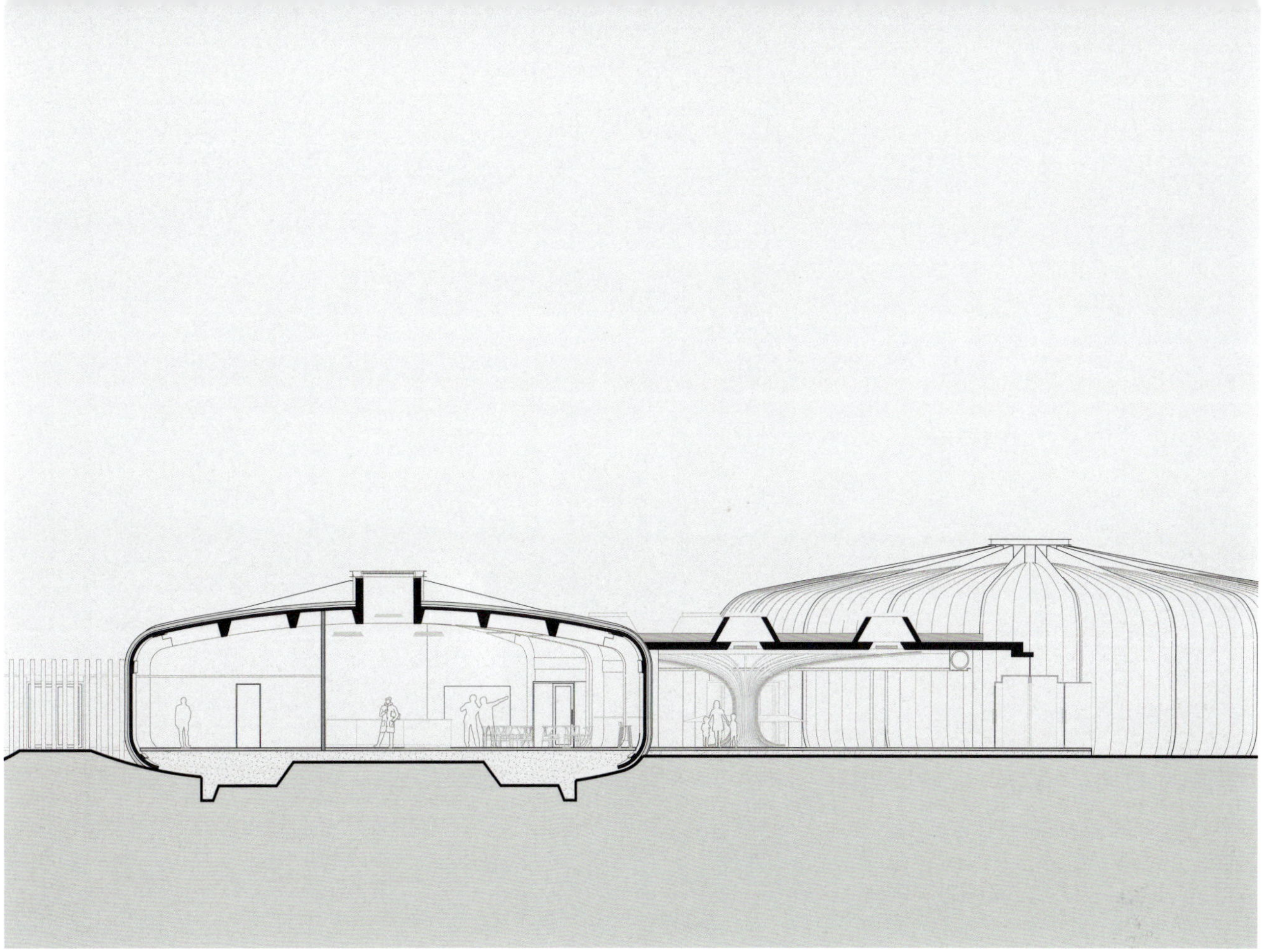

GOOD ARCHITECTURE IS RESOURCEFUL

In a period of increasing climate crisis, resourceful architecture offers sustainable solutions, upholding circular and adaptive practices

Throughout history, humanity has progressed by being resourceful and ambitious. Today, we are experiencing what is known as the "digital revolution," but prior to that there were those of agriculture, industry, and science that changed civilization. Common to each of these periods is the way in which people used resourceful techniques and solutions to address complex problems, be they social or relating to nature. Whether building small shelters or large cities, we have proven adept at modifying and adapting the natural environment in our favor. Until the Wall Street Crash of 1929 rocked the world, the global economic "village" humanity had forged from industry and finance seemed robust. Since then, and following several other economic crises, we now face climate change, and with it even greater uncertainty. As the ancient Greek philosopher Heraclitus knew, the only constant in this world seems to be change.

Today, effective building design must accordingly be adaptive. Given the impact that buildings have on society and the environment, architecture has to have the ability to cope with new requirements, needs, and challenges. According to the "2021 Global Status Report for Buildings and Construction," the construction industry produces 37 percent of all CO_2 emissions, and is therefore significantly responsible for global warming. Although progress has been made in minimizing carbon emissions via technology and the employment of more sustainable design and construction processes, there is still a long way to go. So just what are the latest architectural trends, in terms of design and materials, vying to take things further? And what, precisely, does the "path" to a net-zero architecture look like?

For years, the technification of architecture has meant the incorporation of new prefabrication and/or construction-standardization systems that allow greater efficiency, as well as innovative open-source processes. In each instance, these collaborative approaches say a lot about how we can adapt our designs. At the same time, the employment of Internet of Things technology and automation have also allowed designers to imagine new ways of adapting and reusing existing architecture and materials. These approaches have begun to tackle the construction industry's CO_2 problem, and more is hopefully to come. By expanding its emphasis on design with a circular economy, incorporating passive strategies for thermal comfort, and creating adaptable buildings, architecture is attempting to be resourceful in the face of crisis.

In light of climate change, today the future of building stock—and what can be done with it—is especially topical. "The greenest building is the one that already exists," confirms Carl Elefante, a lead architect at Quinn Evans in the USA, and a board member of the Climate Heritage Network. Indeed, "conversion" and "adaptation" are key words for the architects of today—and tomorrow. Given the changes wrought by these outlooks, the challenge for building design will be to continue to drive down emissions through greater ingenuity.

What should be clear, then, is that today, good architecture is eco-friendly and circular. As such, some of the best examples of resourceful building can be found in works of renovation, from churches that are now libraries, to abandoned warehouses that are now cultural centers. While much has been written on the subject (spanning N. John Habraken's "open building" concept in the 1970s, through studio Adamo-Faiden's contemporary notion of "from mixed-use to diff use"), designers are becoming increasingly aware of how spaces and materials can be reused and modified.

To be sure, we have a lot to learn from the past. If you look through history, there exist construction techniques and uses of local materials that have already proved themselves to be sustainable and have longevity. There, you will also find efficient uses of resources that do not require industrial processing, and those that eliminate the need for long journeys. In some instances, there has even been the use of materials that, at the end of their useful life, can be returned to nature, like adobe and wood.

Undoubtedly, current technology and knowledge can help improve the industry's use of resources, so that some of these strategies can be applied on a bigger scale. Nevertheless, one of the greatest challenges architecture faces is adapting these environmentally low-impact techniques to dense urban contexts. Yet, if history—and projects like those this chapter showcases—are anything to go by, then there is every indication that the industry has the resourcefulness to overcome such obstacles, making this approach not just the "today" of building design, but the future, too.

A TRANQUIL HOTEL REPURPOSED FROM RUINS

DEXAMENES SEASIDE HOTEL

K-STUDIO

KOUROUTA, GREECE

The Dexamenes Seaside Hotel is an industrial restoration piece, located on one of the most beautiful stretches of coastline in the western Peloponnese. The original site was a portside wine-storage and ship-loading zone, built at the turn of the 19th century, and largely untouched since the 1920s. Architects K-Studio were committed to repurposing the derelict industrial assemblage: "From the outset, it was clear that the strong history and raw beauty of the existing buildings should not only be preserved but be showcased in a design that would breathe new life into their walls."

The hotel complex is made up of two sleek modern pavilions connected to the original concrete tank buildings. Each of these is divided into two rows of 10 wine-storage tanks, which are now used as hotel rooms. At approximately 5×6 m (16.4×19.7 ft), the original structures were fortuitously sizable, and are complete with ensuites and shaded patio spaces. The former scrapyard between the two blocks has been reimagined as a "meditative courtyard garden" with a shallow pool that reflects light and provides a cool breeze during the warmer months. Inside the pool is an interactive sculpture made up of two of the original steel drums. This is accessed via thick concrete-slab stepping stones (repurposed from the original structure during doorway construction) that lead guests inside to "experience the way that light and acoustics play over their concave walls throughout the day." In a further homage—with environmental benefits—local grape and currant varieties have been planted in the garden and "will gradually make their contribution to the microclimate and productivity of the hotel."

To harmonize the old and new, the new construction was built using the restrained palette of concrete, steel, timber, and engineered glass. "The new design complements the [original structures'] brutality with elegant interventions and transforms their austere functionality into a place of calm, comfort, and relaxation," say the architects.

The Dexamenes Seaside Hotel repurposes the industrial ruins of a former portside wine storage and shipment-loading zone to create a characterful holiday retreat. The wine storage tanks make up 10 hotel rooms with individual patios (page 227), while the site's former scrapyard acts as a central courtyard. A pool with slab stepping stones leads up to two of the original steel drums (above).

FROM INDUSTRIAL SILO TO NEIGHBORHOOD HAVEN

THE SILO

COBE

COPENHAGEN, DENMARK

In a fledgling Copenhagen neighborhood, a 17-story grain silo has been given a new future as a modern residential and public-serving building. Designed by COBE, The Silo's reinvention is part of a project to transform the industrial area of Nordhavn (North Harbor) into a new district. "By revitalizing our industrial heritage, we discover new potential and highlight historical traces in our cities," says Dan Stubbergaard, COBE's founder. "They represent a built resource. They represent our history."

The exterior of the existing silo has been clad to current standards, with a faceted, climate-shielding facade made of angular galvanized steel that structurally maintains the original shape of the slender building. The steel is a nod to the industrial setting and will patinate and gain its own character over time. "We wanted to retain the spirit of the silo as much as possible, both in terms of its monolithic exterior and majestic concrete interior, by simply draping it with a new overcoat," explains Stubbergaard. "The aim was to transform it from the inside out in such a way that its new inhabitants and the surrounding urban life would highlight the structure's identity and heritage." The interior, meanwhile, has been left as untouched as possible.

The spacious building contains private and public spaces. There are 38 high-ceilinged, single and multi-level apartments with panoramic views of Copenhagen. On the rooftop, encased in glass is a restaurant offering 360 degree views, while the ground floor houses a public event space. The integrative mix of functions ensures that The Silo will play a formative and enduring role in Nordhavn's new history. "Private housing and public functions ensure that the building remains active all day. The public functions at the top and bottom also ensure a multidimensional experience for the various users of the building," says Stubbergaard. "The Silo will be inhabited, but will also be a destination. An urban focal point for the new development at Nordhavn."

The Silo is a former silo turned 17-story mixed-use tower in Copenhagen's revitalized Nordhavn. The building has been brought up to cutting-edge climate standards with a faceted steel cladding that preserves the original slender shape (previous page and opposite, bottom left). Inside, the high-ceilinged apartments and public spaces (above and opposite, top) recall the building's industrial origins, while a glass-walled rooftop restaurant affords panoramic views of the city (previous page).

A FAITHFUL RESTORATION OF A MODERNIST ICON

NEUE NATIONALGALERIE

DAVID CHIPPERFIELD ARCHITECTS

BERLIN, GERMANY

David Chipperfield Architects' shrewdly subtle restoration of Mies van der Rohe's Neue Nationalgalerie balances historical preservation with modern functionality. The building is located in Berlin's Kulturforum (Culture Forum), an arts precinct developed in the late 1960s to provide West Berlin with its own cultural buildings after the city's division. The historic structure is a celebrated icon of modernism, and remains the only European building designed by van der Rohe after his emigration to the United States.

One of Berlin's key galleries, the Neue Nationalgalerie houses a collection of early 20th-century works, as well as temporary exhibitions. "After almost 50 years of intensive use, the listed building required a comprehensive refurbishment," David Chipperfield Architects explains. "The existing fabric has been refurbished and upgraded to current technical standards with a minimum of visual compromise to the building's original appearance." Upgrades include air-conditioning, artificial lighting, and security features, greater accessibility for visitors, improved art handling, and further services including a cloakroom, cafe, and museum shop. The principal division of the space remains true to its history: the iconic main gallery, a light-flooded space on the ground floor, is still used for short-term exhibitions, while the permanent collection is housed underground, adjacent to the new visitor services.

"The key to the complex planning process for this project was finding a suitable balance between monument conservation and the building's use as a modern museum," the architects continue. "The unavoidable interventions to the original fabric within this process had to be reconciled with preserving as much of the original substance as possible." This was done with utmost precision. To repair the reinforced-concrete shell of the building, approximately 35,000 of the building's original components, including the stone cladding and interior fittings, were dismantled and later precisely refitted in their former positions. In spite of the gallery's various new spaces, the end result feels strikingly faithful. "Though the essential additions remain subordinate to the existing design of the building, they are nevertheless discreetly legible as contemporary elements," David Chipperfield Architects explains. "The refurbishment project does not represent a new interpretation, but rather a respectful repair of this landmark building of the International Style."

The Neue Nationalgalerie has been deftly refurbished to contemporary standards without compromising the original modernist design. The underground level houses the permanent collection and new gallery facilities (previous page, bottom, and opposite, top), while the glass-walled street level (above, and previous page, top) acts as the unique backdrop for temporary exhibitions.

WHERE SUSTAINABILITY MEETS THRILL-SEEKING

COPENHILL
BJARKE INGELS GROUP
COPENHAGEN, DENMARK

CopenHill, a new waste-to-energy plant in Copenhagen, rethinks service facilities. The design includes an urban recreation center and an environmental education hub. The massive 41,000 m² (441,320 ft²) plant pioneers what its architects, the Bjarke Ingels Group (BIG), call "hedonistic sustainability," aligning with Copenhagen's 2025 goal to become the first carbon-neutral city.

The Amager Resource Center (ARC) at CopenHill is an innovative waste treatment and energy production site that is economically, environmentally, and socially profitable. Inside, the plant converts 435,000 ton of waste annually into clean energy that will power 150,000 homes. There is also a 600 m² (6,458 ft²) education center for academic tours, workshops, and sustainability conferences.

"CopenHill is conceived as a public infrastructure with intended social side effects from day one," explains BIG. For inspiration, it looked to Amager's industrial waterfront, which had long been used for wakeboarding and go-kart racing. With CopenHill, BIG sought to expand its sports range, offering skiing, hiking, and rock climbing. The plant's machinery was meticulously planned to mimic the shape of a mountain and provide an environmentally friendly, year-round ski slope on the rooftop. At 9,000 m² (96,875 ft²) it is the same length as an Olympic-half pipe and includes a freestyle park, slalom course, lower beginner slopes, and an après-ski bar. Adjacent to the ski slope is a 490 m (1,608 ft) hiking and running trail, designed by Danish landscape architects SLA.

The longest vertical facade hosts an 85 m (279 ft) climbing wall, the tallest in the world. The green roof, meanwhile, boasts innovation of a different kind, having introduced a biodiverse landscape that absorbs heat, removes airborne particle pollution, and minimizes stormwater runoff. This function is enriched elsewhere in the build where the aluminum bricks used on the facade function as planters for a vertical garden.

CopenHill is a waste-to-energy plant in Copenhagen, designed to additionally function as an outdoor recreation center. The machinery inside powers 150,000 homes with clean energy, and was positioned to create a mountain-like incline (opposite, both) for the rooftop ski slope, as well as a hiking and running trail (previous page and below).

A LIGHT-TOUCH RAINFOREST DESIGN

ADMINISTRATIVE HEADQUARTERS OF THE MOSAIC OF JURÉIA-ITATINS CONSERVATION UNITS

23 SUL

PERUÍBE, BRAZIL

The administrative headquarters of the Mosaic of Juréia-Itatins Conservation Units (MUCJI) is an efficient, environmentally friendly building that embodies the organization's ethos. The structure is located in a rain-forest conservation area in Peruíbe, south of São Paulo, Brazil, and houses the state Forest Foundation's administrative, operational, and legal work as well as educational and scientific research. "The building itself symbolizes the values of sustainability and social responsibility which characterize the MUCJI and the foundation's program," explain the architects, 23 SUL. The building marries sustainable, energy-saving materials with a considered layout designed to limit energy consumption in the tropical climate.

To prevent any deforestation, the building sits on an already-cleared site and maximizes space vertically across three levels, including a roof terrace at treetop height. The overarching structure resembles a large pergola that sits above a network of boxy, wooden-framed offices, connected by outdoor walkways. The large, overhanging roof provides the wood with the best possible shelter, defending it against moisture and providing a generous amount of shade. Meanwhile, the open-air corridor that divides the spaces allows air to circulate through each of the floors. "The large eaves of the roof, natural cross-ventilation, and open circulations significantly improve the environmental comfort of the building," explain the architects.

"All construction and operational aspects of the building were designed to generate the least-possible environmental impact. The use of light, durable, and low-waste industrial materials allowed for dry and fast construction," 23 SUL adds. The frame is made with glued, laminated pine called "glulam," a "lightweight prefabrication of renewable source" that lowered reliance on less-sustainable structural materials. The lightness of the framework also meant that the foundation's beams could be supported by small plinths alone, making for an agile construction process. It took one month to assemble and six months to finish the entire building. The internal and external facades of the modular office, meanwhile, are made up of self-supporting laminated panels that fit into the standard wooden frames. Alveolar polycarbonate, the translucent material used, lets in filtered light but is resistant to UV degradation, and is thermally efficient, thereby reducing energy costs.

ADMINISTRATIVE HEADQUARTERS OF THE MOSAIC OF JURÉIA-ITATINS CONSERVATION UNITS

The MUCJI headquarters is a sustainable building, set in a Brazilian rainforest conservation area. The structure is built using light-weight laminated pine, fitted with translucent alveolar polycarbonate panels (above), which are UV resistant and thermally efficient. The frame acts as a large shading pavilion (previous page) over the open rooftop level (opposite, top) and the network of offices, which are bisected by an open corridor (opposite, bottom) that ventilates the work spaces.

A BRUTALIST HIGH-RISE HOME, TRANSFORMED

RIVERSIDE TOWER APARTMENT DUPLEX

STUDIO OKAMI

ANTWERP, BELGIUM

To honor the aesthetic of the brutalist Riverside Tower in Antwerp, Belgium, Studio Okami peeled back a 13th-floor duplex to its concrete shell. The residential tower, located on the bank of the river Scheldt, is an early 1970s design by Léon Stynen and Paul De Meyer. The duplex's radical redesign was dreamed up by its owner, the architect Bram Van Cauter of Studio Okami, which also has its offices in the building.

The conversion saw Studio Okami tear down the internal walls in what was a five-bedroom apartment, creating a capacious layout divided over the 13th and 14th floors. The resulting home has a generous 230 m² (2,476 ft²) floor plan.

On the 13th floor is a spacious, streamlined kitchen and a light-strewn open-plan dining area. "Upon entering the apartment you are greeted by double-height, pivoting windows overlooking the harbor and neighboring forest," explains Van Cauter. "The space is conceived as an entertainment area with kitchen appliances tucked away in a Donald Judd-inspired wall unit."

The 14th floor is accessed via a sculptural spiral staircase in pale blue that was painted and welded in situ by Stielatelier. Upstairs, concrete beams demarcate sleeping, living, and home-office spaces with views of the Antwerp skyline. These center around a bathroom and adjacent utility room.

For the interior to reflect the building's Brutalist exterior, layers of finishing on the walls and ceilings were stripped back to reveal the desired texture of the concrete beneath, to transformative effect. Brick walls were cemented over, and a satisfyingly gritty look achieved by throwing tiny stones into the cement. An artistic solution was henceforth found, and today the existing holes and plugs accommodate the art objects belonging to Van Cauter's partner, the collector Doris Vanistendael.

RIVERSIDE TOWER APARTMENT DUPLEX

The Riverside Tower Apartment Duplex has been faithfully restored to match the residential tower's brutalist design (page 246, top). The lower floor houses spacious dining and streamlined kitchen quarters (page 241), while the upper mezzanine level uses exposed concrete partitions to divide up living, working, and private spaces (above and opposite).

A pale-blue steel staircase (above) was welded in situ and creates a striking contrast within the pale-gray dwelling.

The concrete walls were stripped of their finishing revealing a satisfying patina and useful notches that today are used to hang a collection of artworks throughout the home—to gallery-like effect (opposite, top and previous page).

Back to the Future: Why Refurbishing Matters

With construction accounting for some 40 percent of all CO_2 emissions, it's time to stop building from scratch and start reimagining what's already there

As the late urban planner Jaime Lerner would have it, the future of architecture lies not in building new cities, but in updating those that already exist. It should come as no surprise to hear such a vision expressed by a Brazilian, a denizen of a country whose federal capital, Brasília, was planned and built from scratch between 1956 and 1960, taking the principles of modern architecture to the absolute maximum. Although the renowned planner was talking about urban design, this focus on the city can be equally well applied to the buildings within it, attesting to the fact that some ideas hold true for architecture at any scale.

A grain silo (above both) reimagined as apartments and public facilities.

This is the case with the refurbishment or renovation of existing structures. At a time in history when several regions worldwide are suffering from a shortage of resources, urban densification, and climate change, the most prudent and efficient way of addressing demand for new spaces and facilities is to seek out inventive ways of harnessing what is already there to the utmost effect, while preserving resources for interventions that are absolutely essential.

This strategy makes even more sense when we place it within its wider context. In 2020, the construction sector was responsible for 37 percent of global CO_2 emissions from the manufacture of materials and construction—an all-time high, according to the "2021 Global Status Report for Buildings and Construction."[1] In 2022, the Intergovernmental Panel on Climate Change[2] predicted a 1.5 °C (2.7 °F) increase in the global average temperature over the next two decades, and 4.2 °C (8.4 °F) by 2100 if sufficient measures are not taken, with tragic consequences for the environment and life on Earth. Equally alarming statistics published by research institutes from different countries[3] all seem to point in the same direction: if we want to avoid catastrophic consequences for the planet, we need to take Lerner seriously. We need to stop building from scratch and start revamping buildings in an efficient way.

Although this type of work already accounts for a sizable chunk of what architects do, a number of factors have prevented it from being rolled out on an urban scale. There is still a widespread tendency to view the production chain in architecture in a linear way, with a beginning, middle, and end. In practical terms, architecture begins with the extraction of natural resources—renewable or non-renewable—which are used to realize designs that accommodate people, uses, and functions for a specific period of time, whether this is predetermined or not. This script was followed for a long time, and is still largely pursued to this day, with built-in obsolescence often presaging the ultimate demolition of a building. According to this way of looking at things, natural resources turn into architecture, which in turn ends up as rubble. Some successful examples of architectural renovation and redevelopment projects deal with pre-existing structures that were not originally conceived with their subsequent uses in mind, as with the transformation of 530 residential units in Bordeaux by the French duo Lacaton & Vassal, in collaboration with Frédéric Druot and Christophe Hutin Architecture. Projects of this kind often present architects with complex challenges.

The Dexamenes Seaside Hotel (above, both) was once a wine-storage and ship-loading zone but has been transformed into a hotel by architects K-Studio.

David Chipperfield Architects restored Mies van der Rohe's Neue Nationalgalerie (above, both), sensitively upgrading it to current technical standards.

The overhaul of the Bordeaux development put the economy of means front and center. The form of the structure was transformed, most strikingly through the opening up of the residential units by creating sweeping terraces that run the entire length of the building, while maintaining the original purpose of the development as housing.

Other projects are even more complex due to the need to make more substantial changes to existing structures while remaining mindful of budget constraints. The Silo in Copenhagen is one example. Here, Danish studio COBE converted a 17-story grain silo and a large industrial building into an apartment complex and public facilities. As a way of addressing the inherent incompatibility between the former and latter uses, the architects experimented boldly with form on the facade, so that the final look attested to the radical change that had taken place there.

Projects like those mentioned above are of immense value to the profession, as they move away from a conventional linear approach to architectural production, presenting an ethos of circularity in its place. It might not seem like much, but it takes a lot of sensitivity on the part of architects and urban planners to opt to go back to the drawing board instead of reaching for the wrecking ball. That simple choice has an enormous impact as it creates value, not rubble.

The conventional resources of architecture are also undergoing a paradigm shift. Francis Kéré, winner of the 2022 Pritzker Architecture Prize, immersed a clay brick in water and left it there for five days to prove to his community that the material could withstand the elements and prove a good choice for his debut project, a primary school in Gando, Burkina Faso. "This was a convincing result," recalled the architect in an interview with ArchDaily.[4]

Yet not all buildings can be constructed in rural Gando, nor can they all be made from clay bricks. Instead, they will

In Antwerp, Belgium, Studio Okami undertook the stylish conversion of a duplex apartment in the brutalist high-rise, Riverside Tower (above, all).

increasingly be located in densely populated urban centers where there is a distinct lack of clay, yet an abundance of other material resources used for existing buildings that are now redundant. There is nothing new about this concept, which is often called "urban mining."[5] For that reason, designing buildings that provide scope for adaptation to new uses and functions, and that are easy to dismantle so as to ensure the integrity of the disassembled materials and components, should be an integral part of thinking by architects, engineers, and designers right now, not in the future.

Besides all the benefits of renovating a building or space, such projects also rekindle an issue that has long been at the very heart of architecture: the relationship between form and function. Louis Sullivan's maxim that "form follows function" comes under a certain amount of strain in our example of the grain silo being transformed into a public building, or the former La Samaritaine department store from the 19th century in Paris that morphed into a multipurpose complex with a wavy glass facade at the hands of the Japanese duo SANAA, with LAGNEAU Architectes, François Brugel Architectes Associés, and SRA Architectes. Previously, the form had to follow a specific function, but now it is released from its original obligations and can go on to forge new and sometimes unexpected relationships with a wholly different function, which has to do some adapting of its own, this time to the old form.

In the redeveloped La Samaritaine, the interiors evince a nuanced dialogue with the sturdy, centuries-old metal structures and new skylights supported by a grid of slender metal profiles. The very latest techniques from different periods of history coexist within the same space. On the outside, part of the old building is encased in a diaphanous, reflective skin that forms a new and explicitly contemporary facade for the complex.

"I reinvented the past to see the beauty of the future," said the French poet Louis Aragon in his 1963 book *Le Fou d'Elsa* (*Elsa's fool*). Although he was not talking about architecture, there is much to be gained by adopting this willingness to bring things from the past into the future in discussions surrounding renovation. This is where the true beauty of the act of refurbishment lies: in examining outdated buildings and teasing out elements of quality, whether practical or aesthetic, that we deem to be worthy of standing the test of time so that they can traverse the present and proceed into the future. As to the question of what architecture and cities will look like in the future, the answer may be: they will look more and more like they did in the past.

If we want to avoid catastrophic consequences for the planet, we need to stop building from scratch and start revamping buildings in an efficient way.

SANAA and LAGNEAU Architectes deftly redeveloped La Samaritaine, a former department store in Paris, into a striking mixed-use complex (above, both).

GOOD ARCHITECTURE IS USEFUL

Useful architecture not only fulfills its function but also enhances it, providing other uses and preempting future requirements along the way

The purpose of every architectural creation is to serve people, and good design should be rooted in the specific needs of the individual, group, or community it provides for. Built environments, first and foremost, respond to a set of requirements: how the different spaces will be used, for instance, what they will contain, how they will connect to other spaces, how the user will navigate and experience them, both behaviorally and emotionally. Good architecture prioritizes usability, demonstrating the most intelligent ways of achieving it. Each element of a useful design and concept is purpose-driven, resulting in a careful and deliberate balance between the practical and the creative, form and function, and between utility and aesthetics.

Yet, while architecture must succeed in understanding the needs of its users, it is also important to note that no building or space operates in isolation: the functionality of any built environment is, of course, affected by its context. Therefore, a useful building is one that also responds to the characteristics of its specific location and site, spanning topography, climate, vegetation, and beyond. For example, a building in the midst of a busy city will require a vastly different approach—spatially, materially, and in terms of what it should provide—to one located in a remote setting. By understanding the broader context of the building, the architects can better provide for the inhabitants of the area it occupies, who will coexist and interact with the building on a daily basis. If a building can fulfill not only the requirements of its brief, but cater to the unexpected needs of the place it occupies, so much the better.

There are times when the use of a building is fixed, and from the very early stages of its planning, it is simple to identify the requirements that the structure must meet. Architecture, then, becomes a tool to structure and organize the actions required to revitalize and enhance pre-determined spaces. In the hands of a good architect, an innovation center can become a site where innovation is not only invited, but cultivated; while the incorporation of equitable practices into the various design elements of a social justice center can catalyze positive social transformation on the spot.

In other cases, a building's functions will be more dynamic: the needs constantly changing, or even unknown; the issues to be solved not yet raised. In these cases, architecture has the extra challenge of providing hybrid buildings with structures capable of mixing several interconnected functions, and versatile spaces for the indeterminate future uses and users. From a flexible housing arrangement designed for inhabitants of differing ages and needs, to a striking city carpark with far-reaching potential.

This chapter includes examples of all kinds of useful architecture, spanning the possibility-expanding and the life-enhancing through the multipurpose to the incremental. Good architecture provides imaginative and innovative solutions that go above and beyond in their functionality, integrating the proposed use of a building program into its design while accommodating the surrounding environment and, ultimately, bringing meaning to the community. Useful architecture is one that enables users to connect profoundly with the spaces they inhabit, allowing them to carry out whatever activity is required of them within that space in the most effective way possible. Beyond that, it is architecture that transcends its intended purpose, solving multiple problems to enhance the lives of those that use and interact with it.

A MIXED-USE ICON FOR MIAMI BEACH

1111 LINCOLN ROAD
HERZOG & DE MEURON
MIAMI, FLORIDA, USA

Herzog & de Meuron's 1111 Lincoln Road, known as "Eleven-Eleven," is a mixed-use building that brings together residences, retail spaces, and a creative parking solution in one of Miami Beach's busiest, pedestrian areas. The design reimagines the blueprint of a parking lot, using the interstitial spaces of the stacked, ramp-lined structure to their advantage and opening up various areas for public and private use, complete with panoramic views.

Eleven-Eleven services the Lincoln Road Mall area, a bustling center offering small-scale restaurants and bars, entertainment, commercial retail, and a social overflow to nearby Miami Beach. Occupying a rare pedestrian zone in the otherwise car-dense city, it acts as a pathway between the two, providing the public with space to leave their cars and encouraging them to enjoy the surrounding area on foot.

The development is made up of four elements: an existing 1970s bank building, to which the new mixed-use structure is attached; a two-story building housing the relocated bank; four upper-floor residences that back onto the multi-story parking lot; and, finally, the landscape alley and surface parking lot. On site, there are 300 parking spaces, while various shops and restaurants are split between the ground level and upper section of the building, including a rooftop eatery. With the offering of panoramic views, the architects envisioned the rooftop and upper floors for further use as an event space for film and music videos, fashion shows, and concerts.

The building, according to Jacques Herzog, reinterprets the essence of tropical modernism, imbuing the structure with flair beyond the usual service building and adding to Miami Beach's iconic architecture. Large concrete slabs are set on top of irregular columns that delineate different ceiling heights for the mixed-use building and create a characterful and variegated facade.

As an open concrete structure, Eleven-Eleven is in constant dialogue with its surroundings and invites the community in. By day, the beach-facing building is light and airy; by night, it is illuminated by warm, glowing lights, contrasting the sterile strip lighting traditionally found in dim parking lots. At any time of day, the public can enjoy panoramic views of Miami from each level of the car park, the sculptural interior staircase, or the rooftop restaurant. This, say the architects, lends a "ceremonial feeling" to the building, which at Eleven-Eleven, the public have open access to.

PUBLIC PARKING NOW OPEN

1111 LINCOLN ROAD

1111 Lincoln Road is a mixed-use building that services a bustling commercial center near Miami Beach. Inspired by tropical modernism, the structure proposes a more aesthetically pleasing blueprint for open-access public buildings. Inside, it houses a carpark (previous page and above), commercial center, residence, rooftop restaurant, and event spaces (opposite, top) that all benefit from open views of the oceanfront city.

The ArchDaily Guide to Good Architecture

What's best in architecture today and what's most relevant for tomorrow come together in the first book by *ArchDaily,* the world's most visited architecture website. Drawing on *ArchDaily's* curation of more than 40,000 projects over the past 15 years, it spotlights the most innovative built environments of our age—those paving the way for a better, more sustainable future. Centered around *ArchDaily's* 10 principles of good architecture, the book showcases a rich variety of projects—both built and planned—from a sunken restaurant with subterranean views to a Mediterranean cave transformed into a remarkable residence.

Reflecting a global community of world-shapers, it celebrates the most visionary architects, and introduces bold new talent. It explores the key topics and trends redefining the built environment, marking the forefront of architectural thought and practice today, with an eye on tomorrow.

gestalten
ISBN 978-3-96704-064-7
9 783967 040647

PUBLIC PARKING NOW OPEN

THE MULTIPURPOSE SPACE, MADE SEAMLESS

PAULA RAIA BOUTIQUE AND ATELIER

ISAY WEINFELD

SÃO PAULO, BRAZIL

Behind a beguiling white facade in São Paulo, Brazil, fashion designer Paula Raia's boutique flows seamlessly into her atelier. To find a fitting architectural translation of her design aesthetic, Raia commissioned local architect Isay Weinfeld. The project included renovating the existing building, including a redesign of its entire facade, as well as the creation of new spaces.

The structure and its interior are inspired by the materiality of Raia's work. The minimalist facade is punctuated, at pavement level, with translucent square windows that hint, through glass and gauzy linen, at the warm world inside. "The glass is laminated with fabric, lending transparency to the store interior without overexposing it," explains the architect's studio. The entry hall is an atmospheric vestibule between the street level and the intimate world of the designer. "The entrance features a wall covered in several layers of fabrics with different textures that represent the concept of the garments sold at the store," the architect's studio continues. Like Raia's designs, there is a softness, embodied here in the surfaces, the shades of pink and taupe, the textured, ochre-colored carpet, and the diffused lighting. "This room has abundant natural light shining in from a domed skylight and the facade glass, allowing the existence of a beautiful tree planted on the lower floor. A rustic stone bench rounds out the intended informality of the ambience," they say. This allows the restrained materials to link the mixed-use spaces—natural fabric, carpet, clay textures on the walls, brass and natural rough stones—and a palette inspired by Raia's favored hues.

The building is segmented into four main quarters. On the ground floor is the store, "a wide open space where clients can browse and walk freely among sinuous brass racks, with views onto the inner garden," explains the architect's studio. "The designer wanted to create a sense of freedom for her clients, so we designed it amply bright and light." Housed on a mezzanine level are the storage room and haute couture workshop, where designers and seamstresses work alongside each other. On the lower floor are the technical areas of the prêt-à-porter workshop, plus a space dedicated to alterations and repairs, a pattern-cutting area, and amenities. Finally, Raia's private studio and the design team's room, are tucked away in the outhouse, accessed via a curved path through the inner garden—another vestibule to yet another creative sphere.

PAULA RAIA BOUTIQUE AND ATELIER

Brazilian designer Paula Raia's boutique and atelier pays physical tribute to the work inside. Square windows on the facade contain glass panes laminated with translucent linen (page 262), while the entrance is hung with softly hued fabrics used by the atelier (opposite, top). The palette is continued throughout the boutique and atelier, punctuated by naturalistic elements, such as monolithic seating benches (opposite, bottom) and a courtyard garden (previous page, top).

AN ACTIVE FORUM FOR SOCIAL JUSTICE

ARCUS CENTER FOR SOCIAL JUSTICE LEADERSHIP

STUDIO GANG

KALAMAZOO, MICHIGAN, USA

The Arcus Center for Social Justice Leadership is a study space and meeting center built to support and inspire impactful social change. Part of Kalamazoo College, a liberal arts university in Michigan, USA, the building aims to elevate the struggle for equality from its grass-roots beginnings and support its necessary growth. "Historically, convening for social justice has taken place in the most informal settings, with many of this nation's most important civil rights gatherings, for example, taking place in a church basement, a living room, or even around a kitchen table," explain the architects, Studio Gang. "The challenge of designing a building from the ground up that fosters discussion and renders this work visible and welcome to all is in many ways unprecedented. The Arcus Center for Social Justice Leadership aims to bring social justice topics up from the basement and squarely into public consciousness."

The layout of the building is made up of three wings and, like the cause it supports, focuses on bringing people together. At its heart are the bright and airy social areas: a living room, complete with hearth, as well as a kitchen and dining zone for convivial mealtimes, all intended to stimulate interaction. "Inside, the building's visually open and day-lit interior is designed to encourage 'convening' in configurations that begin to break down psychological and cultural barriers between people and help facilitate understanding," says Studio Gang. Around this open forum, the wings of the building host large, bright lecture halls, meeting rooms, and private study areas—elements that allow the building to address the multifaceted fields of study and advocacy work.

The building honors people and place, inside and out. The center is located at the meeting point of the campus, residential neighborhood, and woodlands. "Its tri-axial plan addresses and unites all three contexts with large transparent facades connected by concavely inflected arcing walls that embrace the interior space," say the architects. Its outer shell is made of wooden masonry, reviving a local vernacular technique, fostering sustain-ability, and allowing the building to gently blend into its environment. "Informed by the tenet that in a socially just world each person's life is valued and their inherent dignity is recognized, the Arcus Center demonstrates that spaces for convening can and should be some of our most powerful," say the architects.

screens
synced
blur the lines
lost
released
humming
secrecy
warped
invisible
bacteria
poisoned river
location
unchecked

The Arcus Center for Social Leadership and Justice is designed to facilitate positive action. At the heart of the building are the integral convening areas (below), while its three wings provide meeting rooms, study spaces, and inspiring lecture halls (opposite, bottom). Located where the campus meets the forest, large windows bring in light and outdoor scenery, while the exterior is clad in wooden masonry, referencing a local vernacular technique (opposite, top).

A SPACE LEFT OPEN FOR INNOVATION

INES INNOVATION CENTER
PEZO VON ELLRICHSHAUSEN
CONCEPCIÓN, CHILE

The INES Innovation Center at the Universidad del Bió-Bió Concepción campus in Chile was built to nurture ideas. In their design for the 2,000 m² (21,528 ft²) building, architects Pezo von Ellrichshausen set out to create a building reflecting the process of innovation in its very structure, composed of wood and concrete in a striking ochre red. To this end, housed inside what the practice deem "an apparently simple, stable, and regular building" is "an unexpected and exaggerated interior."

As well as providing a fluid, open space that could inspire creative thinking, the design sought to cater to the stages of the innovation process, which the architects define as "a creative experience based on a social, collective, and integrated realm, and another, rather individual, intimate and solitary experience." With one glance at the facade, there is a clue to the poetry of the space inside: from the ceiling of the ground floor, a small circular opening grows as it ascends each of the five levels, like the potential of an idea, once explored. Likewise, inside, a vertical, circular passageway forms the building's core. Carved out around it on each floor are spaces that offer a choice between open social exchange or solitary focused research.

The former is catered to by open circular halls fitted with seating areas and views to the outdoors. Like the process of innovation, the private and public research spaces are based on change. These hallway spaces grow smaller on each level while the corners provide wedge-shaped working areas that conversely grow larger. Screened off by curved walls, both visually and acoustically, the rooms can be used according to need—to house exhibitions, workshops, and meetings, for example—and are fitted with multi-purpose tables, window seating, and storage spaces. Unlike traditional academic buildings, there is no formal hierarchy. Instead, the building's democratic layout invites professors, students, researchers, entrepreneurs, and the local community to think, and to innovate, freely.

The INES Innovation Center was built to foster the various stages involved in ideation and exploration. Perhaps its most striking feature is the series of circular voids on each level, visible from the facade (previous page and opposite, bottom right). Inside, the various levels are arranged concentrically around this vertical passageway, providing open, social spaces (above) for exchange and multi-use private working spaces for workshops, meetings, and exhibitions (opposite, top).

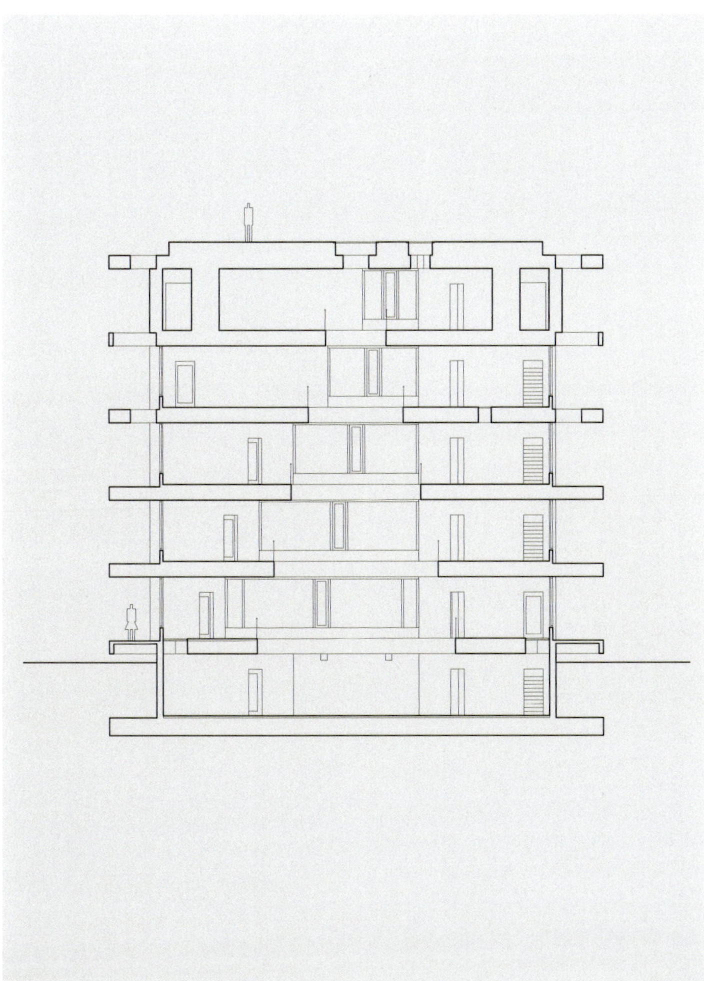

ALEJANDRO ARAVENA: A NO-FRILLS INNOVATOR

Known for his pioneering work on social housing, the Chilean architect challenges the status quo by eliminating the superfluous and the arbitrary

Chilean architect Alejandro Aravena launched his own design studio in 1994, two years after acquiring his degree from Pontifical Catholic University of Chile in Santiago: "It's what everybody does in Chile after graduating: you start your own practice," Aravena says. But it wasn't until 2001 that he founded Elemental, the practice whose work eventually won him the Pritzker Prize—architecture's most prestigious honor—in 2016 and made him a household name in the field.

Sometimes referred to as a "do-tank," Elemental was borne from a period Aravena spent teaching at Harvard in the early 2000s and a felicitous meeting with fellow Chilean, Andreas Iacobelli, then doing a masters in the Kennedy School of Government. Having studied in Chile and later at IUAV in Venice, it wasn't until encountering Iacobelli that Aravena suddenly understood how far removed his architectural education had been from dealing with serious social issues. "Unlike architecture, where you imagine something and then carry that vision from paper or screen to reality," he explains, "here, you imagine a possible outcome, identify forces you don't govern ...

Aravena uses geometry to practical effect. The UC Innovation Center in Santiago (previous page and opposite, top) is made of reinforced concrete with deep-set, rectangular windows that minimize interior heat. The Tourist Promenade in Constitución (above) features geometric lookout points that frame the area's coastal views. Santiago's San Juan de Lampa School (opposite, bottom) is divided into four defined patio spaces, accessed via a single entrance, to control the flow of students.

[with the knowledge that] things may result the way you imagine them indirectly. You understand how small you are and yet you would like to produce big change."

Aravena's desire to produce this change helped develop his unique approach to architectural practice—especially to the world of social housing—through a combination of quality design with an economic framework that encourages residents to personally invest. Much has been written about these projects, but perhaps none more so than 2003's Quinta Monroy in Iquique, northern Chile. With a tiny budget of $7,500 USD per home (including the cost of the land), instead of designing complete-but-mediocre homes, Aravena proposed what has now become his signature idea: incremental design, or "half a good house."

Today, Elemental largely divides its work between three types of projects: social housing, large-scale civic works, and private contracts which lean more heavily on form. While these three elements appear contradictory, Aravena seems to thrive on variety in his work—and perhaps even on the contradictions themselves. Indeed, another seeming contradiction underpins the studio's entire structure. Since 2006, Elemental has been in a unique business partnership between COPEC, a large Chilean energy and forestry company, and the Pontifical Catholic University of Chile. Through Elemental's work on Quinta Monroy, the studio "experienced first-hand that one of the difficulties of social housing is that nobody pays for quality professional time," Aravena explains. So when it came time to find additional funding for the business, COPEC proved an unexpected but ideal partner. "They trusted that our work makes a contribution to society despite the fact that housing had nothing to do with their business." According to Aravena, both COPEC and the university respect Elemental's professional independence while providing knowledge and expertise, as well as the financial capital that has allowed the studio to thrive on its own terms.

Alongside social housing, one of the studio's most significant projects has been its role in the reconstruction of the Chilean city of Constitución following the 2010 earthquake and tsunami. Working alongside other companies such as engineering firm Arup, Elemental consulted local residents on their concerns, and sought to understand local government agencies and departments, particularly their budgets, in order to make the most of available resources. The unexpected outcome was a forest, created to mitigate the effects of future tsunamis and floods, as well as to provide a public park in a city with very little open space. Another result saw waste heat from one of Constitución's large industrial buildings used to heat new public buildings. Aravena's role was diplomatic as much as architectural, and combined his interest in architecture as a cultural act with an informed understanding of the social, political, and economic complexities that underpin any large building project.

Beyond social housing and civic projects, Aravena has designed an innovation center in Santiago, corporate buildings for Novartis and Vitra, and plans for the new Tehran Stock Exchange, alongside numerous publications and curatorial stints for the 2016 and 2021 Venice Architecture Biennales. Elemental has recently been commissioned to design the Art Mill in Doha, Qatar, marking the studio's first large-scale cultural project. Branching out from a stricter focus on social housing and city-making, Aravena remarks that the "cross-pollination of different approaches [has been] crucial for the office." For social housing projects, while Aravena involves himself in conversations around economics, politics, social movements, and the big business of developers and contractors, at the end of the day, he is first and foremost a designer. "We translate the forces at play into form," he says. "When it comes to institutional

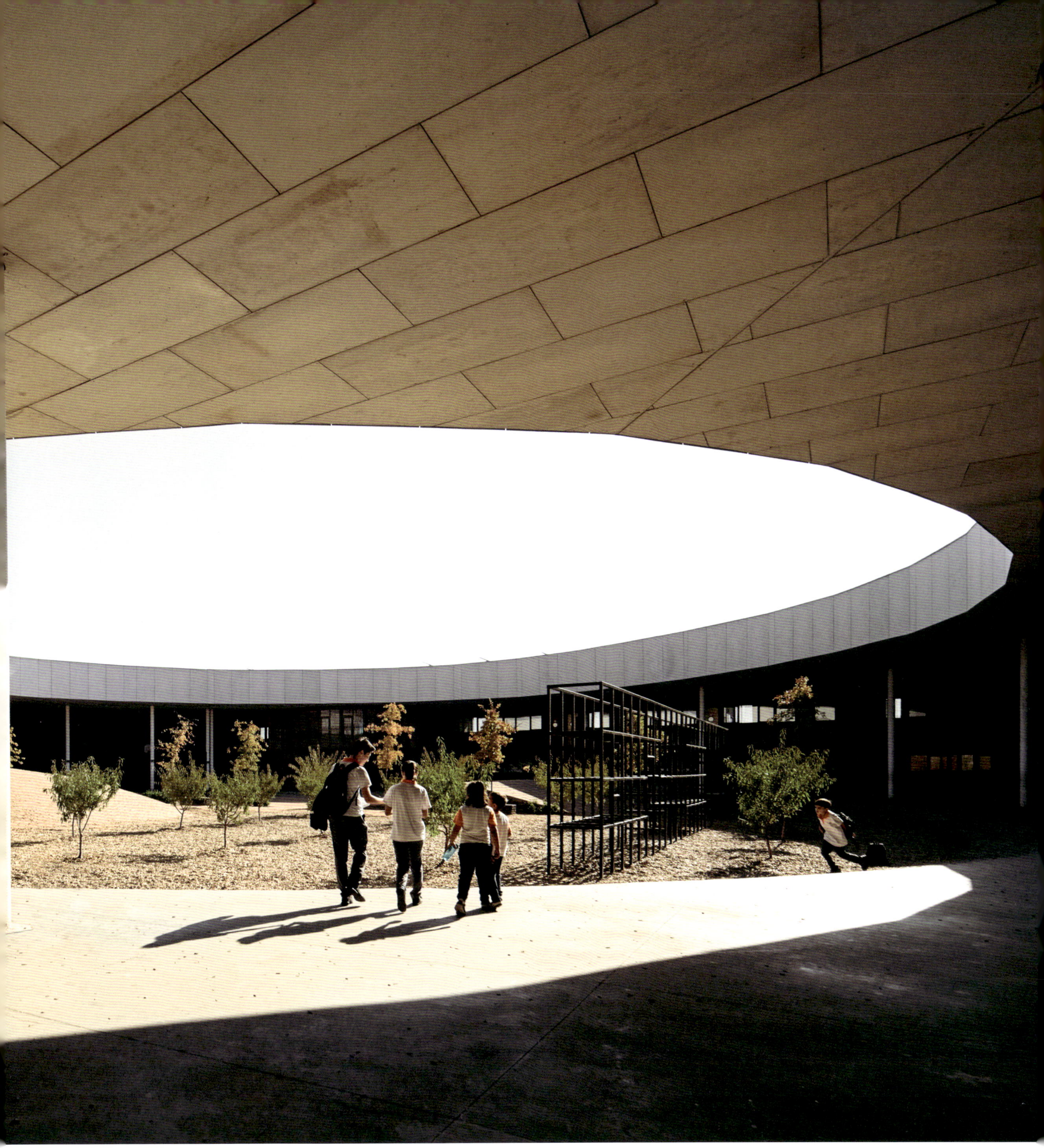

The Ayelén School in Rancagua, Chile (above and opposite) provides children from low-income backgrounds with good, free education, and reimagines the traditional school typology. Aravena placed certain facilities, including the dining areas, computer laboratories, and library, on the school's street-facing facade, inviting public use. While the classrooms and playground lie on the peaceful, interior side. By welcoming the community in, Aravena hoped to encourage an increased sense of safety and connection.

and cultural projects, the same situation applies but the form-making demands are more acute."

This combination of disparate concerns—his navigation of the complex worlds of government bureaucracy and financial scarcity that define the context of social housing, and the demanding form-making required by big-budget private clients—also fuels Aravena's passion for architectural education. He has spoken before of the fact that universities are failing to give architects the training they need to find solutions for the global housing crisis, for instance, and that students aren't taught how to understand political frameworks or economic conditions. "I was educated with the assumption that in order to allow your imagination to fly free, constraints had to be eliminated from the equation," Aravena says. "Over the years, I found that it is exactly the opposite: constraints and difficulties are the reason why creativity and ingenuity is needed." Aravena expresses frustration with the fact that architectural academia has created a kind of parallel universe in which students are encouraged to manipulate contextual circumstances to create "cool results" rather than obtain an understanding of real-world constraints and then design according to context and restrictions.

Aravena's respect for—almost fascination with—constraints and scarcity animates much of the studio's design ethos. Indeed, it is reflected in the name of the practice, "Elemental." Working in social housing, Aravena says, means that "you learn to play in a very tough field, with almost no degrees of freedom, no frills allowed, no fat." While stripping back and reducing is a must in social housing, Aravena says, it is also a desirable quality for almost any project, even if by choice rather than necessity. "By eliminating the superfluous and the arbitrary," Aravena remarks, "projects are better prepared to stand the test of time."

"By eliminating the superfluous and the arbitrary, projects are better prepared to stand the test of time."

Building better futures: the bright and airy El Polígono Sports and Community Center in Illapel (opposite, bottom) is part of the Somos Choapa Program, an alliance between municipalities in Choapa, Chile dedicated to ensuring the sustainable development of the province. With Villa Verde Housing (above and opposite, top) in Constitución, Elemental sought to establish a typology that would further the studio's contribution to social housing by refining its incremental construction model.

Solutions for Living Better, Together

The evolving modes of living environments springing up across the globe are offering bold new approaches to cohabitation, without compromise

In the context of economic, political, and cultural divides, living conditions have instigated one of the most challenging questions in architecture: how will we live together?

Whether through events, public installations, social experiments, or architecture exhibitions such as the 2021 Venice Architecture Biennale, the evolution of domestic living has been a recurring subject among architects, interior designers, and urban planners, inspiring numerous solutions for current and future living environments.

According to the World Bank's Urban Development Overview, it is estimated that by 2030, 60 percent of the world's population will reside in urban areas. Given that the general populace is constantly evolving and relocating, and more workers are migrating to bigger cities, it has become increasingly difficult for people to find an affordable place to live. Some choose to move away from busy city centers, which may mean having to spend more time and money commuting, while some others choose to live minimally in tiny city studios that cater only to their basic daily needs. Along with the change in urban dynamics, the workforce itself has undergone a transformation. With the emergence of startup culture and remote working possibilities, many are opting to abandon conventional nine-to-five jobs—especially those with limited contractual benefits—in favor of freelance projects that allow them to work from almost anywhere in the world, without the need for permanent housing. Meanwhile, those looking to invest in a house are faced with mounting hurdles: nearly 40 percent of millennials in the United States are spending around a quarter of their net income[1] on rent or mortgage payments, compared to the workforce of the 1970s and 1980s.

Casa Torre (above) and Haus 6 (top right): living spaces made to evolve.

The main catalyst for the changes mentioned above is the Covid-19 pandemic, which drastically influenced the way many of us value our physical, mental, and emotional wellbeing, causing rapid and unprecedented change across almost all aspects of life.

So what does a contemporary dwelling look like in the wake of these seminal shifts? Although the basic prerequisites of a house—sleeping, bathing, and kitchen facilities—remain the same, changes in cultural and social habits have birthed multiple new concepts within the traditional house. Keywords like "flexibility," "privacy," "inclusivity," "individuality," and "eco-consciousness" have become driving forces behind the design process, resulting in new residential typologies.

Millennials and members of Generation Z are making different lifestyle choices based on their present reality:

refraining from having large families, for instance, or finding financially viable alternatives to purchasing their own house. As such, micro-living has become one of the world's most rapidly increasing domestic trends. As well as its economic viability, this mode of living has spawned myriad innovative design solutions in terms of spatial organization, storage, and materials. A pertinent example of this is the tiny house, a contemporary housing phenomenon that proves less is more. To maximize on spatial capacity, architects are removing the majority of existing walls from the layouts of such structures, or replacing them with see-through or low-rise partitions to create a more open and interactive space. Interior fixtures are being imbued with new functions, such as integrated shelving units, or hidden storage or seating areas, offering users numerous space-saving solutions. One such example is HAO Design's Block Village in Taiwan, which uses the central staircase as a core, multi-purpose framework that includes a shelving unit, storage, workspace, and partition, spread across both of the project's floors. As for materials, architects are employing reflective and translucent surfaces, bright colors, and natural lighting to create the illusion that these small spaces are much bigger than they actually are.

The BETA Office for Architecture and the City's innovative design is deliberately flexible, smartly anticipating its residents' future requirements.

Three Generation House accommodates two generations of a Dutch family (above, all) within a single, dynamic structure, meeting both parties' needs.

Increasing urban density has long been a critical concern for architects and urban planners, and as cities continue to grow, the question of how to design houses in these densely populated zones has become more prevalent. When properly designed, cohabitation projects can offer affordable and accessible solutions, not just for small families, but for couples, individuals, students, and refugees. By definition, co-living is a community-driven model that accommodates unrelated individuals within the same housing unit. Although the structure itself is one entity, each tenant is given their own private dwelling with essential facilities, which is then supplemented by shared communal spaces such as public gardens, recreational areas, workspaces, and public facilities. La Borda housing cooperative in Barcelona, designed by Spanish architecture firm Lacol, is a good example of a successful cooperative housing model. Awarded the 2022 Emerging Architecture Prize, the project transformed former industrial premises into a structure that could be self-organized by its users to create modest and safe housing that centralizes its value through a collective structure.

Multigenerational living has also found its way back into modern housing structures. As younger generations struggle to afford the cost of living alone, and the elderly find themselves at risk of isolation or neglect, more families are returning to an all-under-one-roof lifestyle. Compared to previous generations, architects nowadays are more aware of the importance of individuality and privacy, and as such are designing spaces that better cater to each demographic while evolving in parallel to their users. These architectural interventions include the incorporation of separate entrances and designated communal spaces situated away from bedrooms, and the reduction of vertical circulation for the elderly.

Lacol consulted with La Borda's future residents when designing the social housing complex. The resulting development is self-organized by its users.

La Borda, Barcelona (above, all), a cooperative housing project by Lacol.

For instance, Amsterdam's Three Generation House, by BETA Office for Architecture and the City, is designed to cater to different generations simultaneously by offering them a two-in-one space that reconfigures to accommodate changing spatial demands over time. Thus residents are encouraged to stay together while being given the privacy and independence they need.

According to a survey by nonpartisan American think tank Pew Research Center, the Covid-19 pandemic has prompted millions of employees between the ages of 30–45, across the global workforce, to quit their jobs in what has been dubbed the "great resignation."[2] Alongside cohorts who were simply made redundant during the pandemic, this demographic represents a significant change in labor habits. Indeed, this change came as little surprise, given that new models of working were already posing a challenge to traditional workplace structures in the years prior to the pandemic—something accelerated by the collective requirement to work from home where possible. In the face of unexpected confinement, residents have had to find ways of integrating office spaces into their floor plans—but not all of them have extra room to spare. Many were forced to squeeze their workspace into a corner of their living room or bedroom, or to transform their dining table into a desk, thereby disregarding ergonomics, privacy, and wellbeing.

For that reason, architects have had to implement a radical modification of how and where people work and live, especially in small-scale housing projects. Seeking to multiply the spatial possibilities in a reduced area, some have used mobile partitions to reconfigure the original spatial division, and allow, for instance, the bedroom to be transformed into a private work area whenever needed. Other solutions include taking advantage of adaptable modular furniture, so that, for example, a hidden desk could be incorporated into a design for use only when necessary; using soundproof and noise-reducing surfaces; allocating workspaces in areas with natural sunlight; and installing ergonomic furniture to further promote productivity and wellbeing within home office spaces.

As to the question of how we will live together today and in the future, the answer should be clear: by revisiting and revamping the very notion of what a home is and does. The traditional house typology that was once dedicated exclusively to living is today being reimagined as a space for work and communal existence, too, in response to the cultural, demographic, and geographic changes taking place around the world. And by looking at the pace at which the world is evolving, it is only a matter of time before yet more novel solutions emerge to redefine the future of our environments for living.

Although the basic prerequisites of a house remain the same, changes in cultural and social habits have birthed multiple new concepts within the traditional house.

All La Borda's residential units overlook a central courtyard (opposite, bottom left), affirming the spirit of collective ownership and active participation.

AN INTERGENERATIONAL HOME BUILT TO EVOLVE

THREE GENERATION HOUSE
BETA OFFICE FOR ARCHITECTURE AND THE CITY
AMSTERDAM, NETHERLANDS

Three Generation House was built for an extended family unit across different stages of life, bringing them together in an adaptive home that is sensitive to their varying requirements. Designed by BETA Office for Architecture and the City, the project was commissioned by two generations of a family who, up until this time, had lived as separate households. One half was a young family, already residing in Amsterdam, while the other were their grandparents, a couple looking to move from the countryside back into the city.

In their design process, BETA contemplated how best to care for different generations. "For this mini-apartment building, a concept was devised capable of accommodating changing spatial demands over time," the architects explain. The resulting 450 m² (4,844 ft²), multi-level building is separated into two distinct zones. The top of the apartment, with its views across Amsterdam, is home to the senior couple. The easy-access design boasts level floors and is serviced by an elevator. The lower portion of the building, meanwhile, houses the young, working family, and is fitted with an office and direct access to the garden where the children can play. On each of the floors are generous south-facing balconies overlooking the outdoor space and floor-to-ceiling, triple-glazed windows that let in light and retain the sun's warmth. The northern, street-facing facade, by contrast, is mostly closed in order to thermally insulate the building and block out urban noise. "In-between the two contrary facades, the building's plan undergoes a gradual transformation, from compartmentalized in the north, to open-plan and structured with free-form elements towards the south," BETA explains. The efficiency of the building is bolstered by structural walls made of concrete masonry wrapped in high-grade thermal insulation. The interior is characterized by these bare concrete slabs offset by warming timber elements such as inbuilt cabinetry.

Over time, the building, like its occupants, will grow. This is made possible by the positioning of the vertical stairwell at the heart of the building. Sculptural at its base on the lower levels, it opens up what the architects call "spatial voids" on the upper floors, allowing for a "surplus floor" to be combined with either apartment. It is generally used as a guest space for the top apartment but can be adjusted, according to the family's need, to form part of the lower apartment.

BERG

THREE GENERATION HOUSE

Three Generation House is built to flexibly house an extended family as they move through life. The five floors are each fitted with a south-facing terrace and comprise a young family home on the lower two floors (above and opposite, top), and a flexi-use middle floor that adjoins the upstairs apartment for the grand-parents (opposite, bottom). All are linked by a sculptural central staircase in bright yellow (above).

GOOD ARCHITECTURE IS DESIRABLE

Desirable architecture delights and surprises, while acknowledging its social and environmental responsibility

Architects are responsible for juggling countless factors, from structural loads, circulation, and deadlines to budgets, local constraints, and client requirements. In addition, they are expected to create desirable buildings, conjuring a pleasant environment for those they serve. It's a lofty challenge—the successful combination of the artistic and the utilitarian—and one which has been debated for thousands of years. The 1st-century BCE Roman architect Vitruvius stated that, in order to attain what he considered beauty (e.g. bringing pleasure to all), an architectural project should be based on the triad *firmitas, utilitas,* and *venustas. Firmitas* means that the building must be stable; *utilitas* means that it must fulfill its intended function; and *venustas* refers to its beauty. Although the latter was considered an architect's main role for many years, Vitruvius believed that to be truly beautiful, a building must also possess utility and an appropriate structure.

Symmetry, rhythm, and proportion. This is what defined classical architecture, considered the ideal model in Western civilization, with its balance of the attractive with the practical. Thus while buildings were made with gables, ornaments, and decorative elements, these structures were only considered beautiful if they served a purpose, too. (Think of Rome's Colosseum, an elaborate amphitheater for gladiatorial contests, or Athens's Parthenon, an awe-inspiring shrine to Athena).

Since then, the concept of what a beautiful building is has changed, with some styles, such as gothic, eclecticism, and art nouveau, going in and out of fashion, and others proving short lived. Nevertheless, while the idea of "art for art's sake" might have caught on in galleries, building design has remained true to the idea that beauty and practicality go hand-in-hand, whatever style is *à la mode*. Following the Second World War, for instance, the rupture brought about by modern architecture in Europe's reconstruction rejected ornamentation. This was when Louis Sullivan coined the phrase "form follows function," and Le Corbusier created at Villa Savoye in Poissy. Considered the refined embodiment of the modernist master s architectural system, it is an ode to function and austerity with its straight shapes, white walls, and hard surfaces. Despite renouncing decoration while seemingly obsessing over function, modernist architecture did not in fact dismiss the notion of aesthetic pleasure. Instead, it created a new style that was, over time, incorporated by architects around the world.

Mies van der Rohe is a good case study. A precursor of the International Style, he claimed that "less is more," and removed everything he considered unnecessary from his buildings. Although it is not certain whether he also coined the phrase "God is in details," what can be affirmed is that modern architects have since designed details as aesthetically as possible. As some theorists like to say, in modernist architecture the notion of the ornament was relegated to the details or small elements of buildings. These do not always just solve functional or technical issues, but can be used to properly finish corners or hide something undesirable. In any case, what is clear is that, rather than abandoning the idea that buildings should bring people joy, van der Rohe and co. shifted the coordinates of what that meant for their generation.

What these cursory historical glances hopefully demonstrate is that styles of beauty are intrinsically linked to their periods. A society's tastes refer to and reflect its thoughts and repertoires, expressing convictions, knowledge, morals and politics, and even class. To be desirable, in a compact definition, is to be "wanted or wished for as being an attractive, useful, or necessary course of action." And the desires of any given society are expressed through its buildings, including what it finds pleasurable.

Enjoyment, however, does not mean merely boundless joy, and if today's architecture is to be considered beautiful in the future, it must go beyond mere aesthetics—or even the Vitruvian triad. In an increasingly complex world dealing with worrying global issues, the ideal of a desirable architecture must now include responsibility and ethics. This means incorporating, in addition to pleasant aesthetics and adequate functionality, concepts of sustainability, accessibility, durability, and social benefit.

When designing, the architect must also take into account that, unlike a painting or a play, architecture carries within itself a public quality. That is, a building impacts the lives of many more people than just its residents or users, and will last decades or even centuries. The act of designing requires enormous responsibility. And as the buildings in the following chapter demonstrate, a truly desirable architecture balances looks with utility. If it is also able to captivate and thrill, on top of all the other considerations, even better. Which is to say that, in terms of aesthetics, the beauty of architecture goes much deeper than the facade.

A BRIDGE BETWEEN ART AND THE CITY

JISHOU ART MUSEUM

ATELIER FCJZ

JISHOU, CHINA

The Jishou Art Museum in China is a regional museum that slots into the Hunan-region city of Jishou's traditional old town, functioning as both a cultural center and a pedestrian bridge across the river Wanrong. The central location was proposed by its architects, Atelier FCJZ, who opposed the municipal plans to build in a developing zone outside the city. "We believed that a cultural facility should be easily accessible," they explain.

The museum's dual form encourages an incidental discovery of art. "Typical contemporary cultural institutions in China are treated as freestanding monuments, far away from communities," say the architects. "Here, we hope that people will not only make a special trip to see art but will also encounter it on their way to work, to school, or to shop." As such, their building is deliberately "inserted into the urban fabric," bridging the shops, restaurants, hotels, and residences that line the embankment. "The front entrances of the museum on both riverbanks are part of the mixed-use street walls," they expand.

The building's striking form references the long tradition of the *fengyu qiao*, or wind and rain bridge, unique to China's mountainous region. These covered bridges also had a dual usage: they were used as places of rest for travelers, with attendant vendors trading from their stands. "We introduced art as a new program on a covered bridge while maintaining pedestrian traffic, translating the formal language of the *fengyu qiao* into a modern one," explain the architects.

The contemporary iteration sees two bridges stacked on top of each other. On the lower level, an open steel-truss structure, lies the pedestrian thoroughfare, while the upper level, made of cast-in-situ concrete, houses the gallery. The gallery's main hall sits in-between the two, enclosed within glazed walls and a tiled shading system. The museum amenities, meanwhile, including its shop and cafe, feature at either end.

The bridged form of the Jishou Art Museum straddles the river Wanrong in China's Hunan province (previous page), and is inspired by the traditional form of the region's historic covered *fengyu qiao* (wind and rain bridge). The upper level houses the light-flooded gallery space (opposite), while the lower public crossing, accessed on the old-town street level through a subway-like entrance (above), offers the public the daily opportunity for a chance encounter with art.

A VERDANT HOME FOR ALL TO THRIVE

CORNWALL GARDENS HOUSE
CHANG ARCHITECTS
BUKIT TIMAH, SINGAPORE

Cornwall Gardens House in Singapore unites generations of family in a verdant, communal home founded on well-being. "This house is intended for multi-generation living. The client wanted an 'open home, a cool tropical paradise for the family,' encouraging their children to 'raise their families here when they grow up,'" explain the designers, Chang Architects. Their approach harnesses the life-improving qualities of plant-life. "Designed with an 'I-Thou relationship' with nature [a 20th-century religious philosophy conceived by Martin Buber], the family and nature share the same breathing space," they explain.

At the entrance, the desired tone is set by a welcoming koi fish pond and waterfall, whose soothing sounds resonate gently throughout the home. The multilevel structure is built around a core courtyard that houses a natural, stone-ringed swimming pool, and links a program of indoor and outdoor spaces. Balconies and walkways, planted with various cascading plant species, lead to the various living quarters and communal spaces including landscaped decks and rooftop gardens. The tiered structure uses every opportunity to house greenery, creating a thermally efficient home for the tropics. "Working with the existing terrain, built-ups that contributed to the site coverage are utilized as planters for tropical fruit trees, to cool ambient temperature, and to insulate the interiors," explain the architects. The planters have the added benefit of catching and recycling water to irrigate the substantial plant life.

This harmonious program has brought life of every form in. "The setting provides daylight, natural ventilation, and passive cooling. It offers an ecologically friendly environment that promotes general wellness for all," explain the architects. "This house has become a popular gathering place for the owners' extended familiy and friends, and it has also attracted a host of biodiversity, from bees and butterflies to squirrels."

Cornwall Gardens House is a lush multi-generational home that fosters wellbeing. The cavernous terraced roof (above) forms a garden that cascades into the central courtyard with its natural swimming pool (previous page). Its work is continued by the garden beds attached on the balconies and walkways at each level (opposite, top). Meanwhile, a trickling waterfall greets the entrance, resonating its calm soundtrack throughout the cavernous house (opposite, bottom).

AN ARBOREAL BUILDING TO CALM AND CONNECT

TREE-NESS HOUSE
AKIHISA HIRATA
TOSHIMA, JAPAN

Tree-ness House is an arboreal-inspired apartment complex in Toshima, Tokyo, that bridges the urban with the natural world. Designed by studio Akihisa Hirata, the building references the complex form of a tree, from its trunk and branches to its leaves. "As with the tree, we tried to create an organic architecture that could be formed by a hierarchical combination of different parts," explains Hirata.

The main structure makes use of the long but narrow site and is formed of offset stacked concrete boxes, the positioning of which naturally opens up voids in-between. Trees have been planted in these cavities to create "an organic whole, breathing in the surrounding environment like a tree." The three-dimensional facade, with its greenery and terrace spaces, is part of the architect's efforts to focus equally on the building's exterior and interior, playfully furnishing the building with a vertical garden. Fitted with outdoor staircases, when viewed from the side, the building, with its flurry of outside activity, curiously resembles an architectural cross-section. This inversion is in line with the architect's desire to upend traditional urban living structures and connect city-dwellers with their environment. "I intended to create a futuristic and savage architecture that awakens human animal instincts in which the inside and outside are reversed multiple times," says Hirata.

The building provides its residents with a balanced lifestyle. While social quarters such as living rooms and dining rooms face outwards, bringing light in and acting as transitional spaces to the outdoor areas, the interior houses calm, private environments, including generous bathrooms and bedrooms. These inner sections are warmed by wooden elements and illuminated by the cavities created in the box-stacking design. With its innovative program, the building pushes the envelope of urban builds in densely populated Tokyo, prioritizing access to nature and spaces of calm for city-dwellers.

Tree-ness house brings organic inspiration into the urban Tokyo context. The structure is made of offset, stacked cubes with outdoor terraces that appear like cross-sections of the indoors in a whimsical inversion (previous page and opposite, top). Trees and greenery grow from deep planters and rooftop plots, bringing life to the gray facade and casting views of nature inside the homes (opposite, bottom).

ISAY WEINFELD: A CREATOR WITHOUT CONFINES

From scenic rural landscapes to high-rise office blocks, the São Paulo-born Brazilian architect never shies from a challenge

Brazilian architect, filmmaker, furniture and set-designer Isay Weinfeld was born in 1952 in Bom Retiro, a Jewish neighborhood of São Paulo, where he and his younger brother were raised by their parents. Located close to the South Atlantic, São Paulo is one of the world's most populous cities and boasts its own rich architectural heritage. Among its iconic buildings are the 1929 Martinelli skyscraper, the colonial-style Pátio do Colégio church that marks where Jesuit priests founded the city in 1554, and Oscar Niemeyer's sinuous Edifício Copan. Yet it was Weinfeld's Portuguese language teacher who first tapped into his creative interests with a passion for cinema. The architect explains, "Once a week he would rent a movie and screen it to the students in the school auditorium. It was on one of those occasions I watched Ingmar Bergman's *Wild Strawberries,* which affected me deeply." It was, however, a quotidien encounter with architecture that triggered his first thought experiments in this field. "The earliest memory I have of a contact with architecture was at 13 or 14, when I saw the scale model of a development at a sales stand and kept

With his client-based approach, Weinfeld avoids easy categorization, whether designing bookstores, offices, hotels—like the Fazenda Boa Vista (opposite, bottom)—or homes. The 360° Building (previous page) is a towering residential high-rise, made up of lofty apartments replete with their own capacious yards. AB Apartment (above) offers a sleek update on Brazilian modernism for a private client, while Casa Grecia (opposite, top) is a stunning house and garden made up of multiple spaces.

envisioning people living in those spaces, sleeping, reading, walking…"

Weinfeld's portfolio of work is defined only by its breadth of material and scale. When it came to selecting a college major, and a path for further education, a young Weinfeld was taken by the opportunity to pursue a creative life with the potential to thrive professionally. He explains, "I think I chose architecture [at São Paulo's Universidade Presbiteriana Mackenzie] because it was a profession that would allow me at once an established, regulated trade, and an education with an artistic foundation, in which I could seek to express myself in different ways. From an early age, I have always been interested in vastly different subjects and tried several paths before architecture—visual arts, performance, cinema. Thus, architecture is a result of happenstance in my life."

Reflecting on both his own academic experiences and patterns he has observed in his almost half-century as a professional, Weinfeld cites experimentation, freedom, and abstract thinking as being key to creative and architectural education: "I believe colleges should allow students to exercise their imagination without real-world boundaries. Laws, timelines, and price estimates are all issues they will not be able to escape in their professional life, so at school I feel they should take wing, exercise their creativity, and experiment to the maximum."

Weinfeld says he is "averse to specialization, to the idea that I know how best to solve a certain program or issue." The spectrum of objectives and desires represented in his work is testament to this. He has never resigned himself to a corner of architecture, or settled into a niche, despite this being a tried-and-tested way to sustainably procure work for so many architects. In 2011, Weinfeld completed work on Livraria da Vila, a 766 m^2 (8,245 ft^2) commercial bookstore in his home city of São Paulo. Meanwhile, around the same time, he was working on the scenic, 3,995 m^2 (43,000 ft^2) Fasano Las Piedras Hotel in Punta del Este, Uruguay. In 2012, the architect turned his attention to the unique challenge of designing an equestrian center clubhouse at Fazenda Boa Vista. Jumping genre again, this time to urban development, Weinfeld completed work on the Santos Augusta office building in 2017, which sits among a high-rise cluster with striking views of São Paulo. "I need the challenge, the excitement of trying something new, of experimenting out of my comfort zone with something I never did, and to surprise myself—for the better and the worse, because we are always subject to hits and misses."

What makes Weinfeld's projects unique, both to him and in their own right, is his client-first approach to every project. Before assigning his own vision to a brief, he sits down with his client to discuss theirs. He explains, "Clients are always my primary inspiration. As a rule, at my first meetings with a client, when they start describing their wants and designs for the new project, I start day-dreaming and let them speak, while I think about what I will do after the meeting. I think about last night's dinner, about the demonstration I saw on TV. I concentrate again, and what they are saying then reminds me of a scene from months ago. I remember a dance performance I saw, a dead dog hit by a car. I remember to call a friend I have not seen in weeks and documents that are still to be signed. These are facts parallel to the conversation, but somehow connected to it, that will make me start the project that will somehow turn out just like that client." When tasked with imagining a new abode in São Paulo's fashionable Jardins district for a young Brazilian-French couple, Weinfeld created a bright and informal space to accommodate both the playfulness of their three children and the beauty of their Brazilian art collection. The Centro Cultural do Instituto Ling in Porto Alegre, Brazil, was designed by Weinfeld and completed in 2014. It holds exhibitions, concerts and performances, so the architect designed each section along the gallery to open

Fasano Las Piedras (above, following page top): an awe-inspiring hospitality complex in the Uruguayan city of Punta del Este. The project encompasses private homes, hotel bungalows, and amenities including a spa and equestrian center. Low-lying rectangular volumes abound, as does a rich array of covetable materials, hues and textures, inside and out. Within São Paulo's Oito Building (opposite), a yellow, spiral staircase demonstrates Weinfeld's playful use of color and form.

differently to the exterior, in order to control the incoming light, according to its intended use.

When asked about his influences, Weinfeld's architectural references include only Italian-born Brazilian modernist architect Lina Bo Bardi and Mexican architect and engineer Luis Barragán, whereas creatives from other fields seem to pour from his mind. From the music industry, he recognizes Kanye West and Radiohead, while Swedish director Ingmar Bergman, Italian auteur Federico Fellini, and French mime, actor, and screenwriter Jacques Tati all represent the world of filmmaking. Commenting on his interdisciplinary interests and influences, he says, "It was [Stanley] Kubrick that led his career the way I wish I would lead mine. He shot so many different genres—war movies, romantic movies, thrillers, sci-fi movies—and still, it was always a Kubrick movie. I do not like to see myself constrained by the boundaries of the profession as an architect, and that reflects directly in the portfolio of our office, where we design everything from homes to buildings, from hotels to stores and restaurants, from a center for the homeless to cultural institutes; as well as furniture, scenography, exhibition designs, and beyond."

It is the comfort, needs, and desires of his clients that define Weinfeld's work. He vehemently rejects the idea that demonstrating a specific set of skills should validate his designs, "I never knew how to sketch by hand. No one ever told me it was possible to be an architect without that skill. Maybe that is not truly possible. Maybe I am not truly an architect." In a 2011 interview, he alluded to the fact that he would never live in any of his projects. He adds, "I said I would hate to live in the houses I designed not because I do not like them, but simply because I did not design them for me. A house project is always tailor-made, specific to a family's very particular needs. It considers each family's very unique daily routines, tastes, dreams, idiosyncrasies, dynamics, so they are not necessarily suited to me. Yet, since 2014, I have been living in a unit in a building I designed and I am very happy because this, indeed, was tailored to my life."

"I need the challenge, the excitement of trying something new, of experimenting out of my comfort zone with something I never did, and to surprise myself."

For the Azul Building in São Paulo (opposite, bottom), Weinfeld conceived a residential project made up of three mixed-use structures. Prioritizing ventilation, natural light, and pleasing views, theyare connected by a captivating, bright-blue walkway. Casa das Filgueiras (above) is a covetable São Paulo home that foregrounds harmonious juxtapositions throughout its design: between indoors and outdoors, the natural and the manmade, between light and dark tones, and smooth and rugged textures.

A JOYFUL THOROUGHFARE FOR URBAN SHANGHAI

HENDERSON CIFI TIANDI
ATELIERS JEAN NOUVEL
SHANGHAI, CHINA

Linking the Ma Dang and Dan Shui thoroughfares, the passageway formed by Shanghai's Henderson Cifi Tiandi building is known as The Street of 1,000 Red Jars. Combining offices and commercialv units, the building was created by Paris's Ateliers Jean Nouvel, and sits in the former French concession district of Huangpu. As the site runs an entire block, the architect Jean Nouvel admits he could not resist linking the streets with an "urban and commercial passageway"—and the idea was born.

The passage references the district's varied history, equally inspired by its French concession-era architecture as it is traditional Chinese shopping streets. In China, red is a symbol of luck and happiness, lending the color's on-site abundance added significance. According to Nouvel, the building evokes its "vanished surroundings that have been completely reimagined and are new and modern."

The red passageway breaks up the building's muted facade and calls out to be discovered from the adjacent street. Multiple bridges link the two-winged structure, offering utility and visual charm. Plant pots overflowing with greenery line the many levels of the passageway and the exterior facade, bringing the outdoors in with cheering results and offering residents privacy. "Shadowplays produced by the adjustable slats of the blinds, in front of windows bordered by huge flower pots, play on the mystery of presences and activities," expands Nouvel, "while inventing a landscape of vegetal friezes in the colors of the season and of the different flowers." The development invites activity, fulfilling its intention. "The complementarity between the shops facing each other, the activities of the offices, and the restaurants up under the roofs, creates a familiar and naturally animated street, setting pleasing walks as a target and offering an inviting new itinerary between Ma Dang and Dan Shui streets," says the architect.

Known as "The Street of 1,000 Red Jars," the passageway that bisects Shanghai's Henderson Cifi Tiandi building (previous page) is a modern interpretation of the traditional Chinese shopping street. The thoroughfare, colored in lucky red and bursting with diverse plant life (above), is a joyful departure from the urban center, providing pedestrians, office-workers, and lunch-goers with daily delight.

A KINDERGARTEN THAT IGNITES IMAGINATION

YUECHENG COURTYARD KINDERGARTEN

MAD ARCHITECTS

BEIJING, CHINA

Beijing's YueCheng Courtyard Kindergarten is a free-flowing space where children can play, learn and imagine. The large 9,275 m² (approx. 100,000 ft²) kindergarten was designed by MAD Architects, and provides preschool education to 390 children aged from 18 months to six years old.

In conceiving the design, architect Ma Yansong considered what a kindergarten should provide a child, as well as what a child would want in the space. "It must always make kids feel freedom and love," he says. Fitted with safety fencing, the rooftop doubles as a playground with a chromatic palette, a contrast to the city's blues and grays. "The undulating 'caving' topography of the roof forms a Martian landscape of sorts, enticing children to interact with it and each other," explains MAD. The low-lying kindergarten structure connects children to their history and wraps around an 18th-century Siheyuan courtyard, typical of Beijing. "When combined with the ancient courtyard, old trees, and infinite sky, a surreal environment inspires children to think, reflect, and chase endless possibilities," says MAD. Three new courtyards were built around the site's trees, bringing light and ventilation into the indoor teaching spaces, while passage-ways offer access to the rooftop via slides and stairs.

The building's interior is set low to frame a child's worldview. The facilities are playfully practical: the lobby is designed as a theater, where the stage doubles as an entrance to an indoor playground, which in turn, can be used to host art and sports events. There is no rigid floor plan inside, with communal spaces and mixed-age learning groups demarcated by curved structural walls. "The 'borderless' learning space, ubiquitous reading environment, and curriculum focusing on learning through exploratory play, not only enriches the interaction between children but also allows teaching and learning to take place in an optimal atmosphere," MAD explains.

YUECHENG COURTYARD KINDERGARTEN

The YueCheng Courtyard Kindergarten is designed to encourage free, imaginative play. The low-lying building encloses traditional courtyards, visible via floor-to-ceiling glazing, and storied trees, around which new courtyards have been created (opposite, bottom, and previous page, bottom left). The undulating rooftop acts as a giant playground, with slides connecting down to the ground-level courtyards (above and opposite, above).

ArchDaily's Staff Picks

The *ArchDaily* team talk all things architecture, from pet peeves and favorite details to dream homes and extraordinary interiors

Clara Ott
PROJECT MANAGER

Which far-flung building would you plan a vacation around? I would go all the way to Casa Wabi, on the outskirts of Puerto Escondido, Mexico. This series of buildings is more than just an art foundation: it combines a mission to promote social commitment through art with a blend of Mexico's vernacular pre-Hispanic heritage, and abstract contemporary proposals by the greatest names in contemporary architecture. Visiting such an astounding location on the Mexican coast, featuring works by Tadao Ando, Álvaro Siza, Alberto Kalach, Kengo Kuma, and Ambrosi Etchegaray, is definitely worth the trip.

If you could live in any building, where would you choose? I would live in direct contact with nature in Japanese architect Ryue Nishizawa's house in Ochoquebradas, Los Vilos, Chile. What I like most about it is how perfectly balanced it is: the roughness of the cut cliffs and the fierce ocean, the refinement of the undulating concrete roof, and the transparency of the glass all result in a perfect combination of protection and exposure—the house practically floats over the rugged coastal landscape.

A favorite architectural moment/scene in cinema? The joy in Ariadne's eyes in *Inception* the first time she is guided into a dream with the task of designing its architecture. Her eyes sparkle as she innocently discovers what her mind is capable of coming up with, and the possibilities that arise as she playfully rediscovers architectural elements. I think it is the cinematic version of every architect's relationship with architecture.

Who takes the best photographs of architecture? I admire the work of Julius Schulman, who photographed most of the Case Study Houses in California in the 1950s. Shulman paved the way in terms of capturing not only architecture, but also its surroundings and, more importantly, its essence. His images boast a carefully staged domesticity, often including a house's inhabitants within the frame. He shot with multiple exposures, turning lights on and off, and made use of flashes to achieve his striking pictures.

Casa Wabi in Puerto Escondido, Tadao Ando's first project in Mexico.

Fernanda Castro
CONTENT DIRECTOR

Name a building that evokes a special memory for you. The Teshima Art Museum by Ryue Nishizawa in Japan has a very special place in my memory. The whole experience starts when you arrive at the island of Teshima. It is a pilgrimage of various routes, trains, boats, and walks. Upon going into the museum, the design stimulates you to enter into a deep state of meditation. It's all about the way architecture integrates with the surrounding landscape—air flow, sounds, and echoes. All this together makes the whole experience much more meaningful. I recommend visiting both the islands of Teshima and Naoshima, where you will discover works by an array of artists, from James Turell to Claude Monet, and experience buildings by Tadao Ando, SANAA, and Hiroshi Sambuichi, among others.

If you could live in any building, where would you choose? When I visited London, I had a chance to visit the Barbican and it exceeded all my expectations. It is truly one of the most remarkable examples of brutalist architecture in its imposing scale, but, at the same time, perfectly embraces public space. Living in a historical place that integrates cultural, educational, and public space programs so well would be a privilege.

Name the building/s that made you fall in love with architecture. I have not had the chance to go there yet, but Ricardo Bofill's La Fábrica is definitely the building that has never ceased to surprise and inspire me. An old abandoned cement factory on Barcelona's outskirts has been converted into one of the most elegant, mysterious, and delicate architectural works ever, maintaining and respecting the original industrial structure and scale. La Fábrica serves as a reminder that architecture can be one of the most sublime forms of art.

Teshima Art Museum, a gallery in Japan housing a single artwork.

Which far-flung building would you plan a vacation around? When it comes to remote places, the Remota Hotel in Chilean Patagonia is the next destination on my travel list. Designed by Chilean architect Germán del Sol, the hotel merges into the landscape in a respectful way, almost blending in with the nearby meadow and surrounding geography. It is a place that prioritizes the contemplation of landscape as its main experience.

David Basulto

FOUNDER & EDITOR IN CHIEF

Which far-flung building would you plan a vacation around? One of my favorite remote locations to plan a whole experience around is Naoshima Island in the Seto Inland Sea, Japan. Two museums designed by Tadao Ando house unique artworks and sublime experiences by Walter de Maria and James Turrell, among others, that justify scheduling plane, train, ferry, bus, and bike rider to reach this remote location. Ando also designed a hotel on the island that is an experience in itself, thanks to its extensive art collection that you can experience during your stay—it's almost like sleeping inside a museum. It is just a ferry away from Teshima Island—home to a surreal museum by Ryue Nishizawa and artist Rei Naito—where a drop of water becomes the centerpiece. Moreover, the Setouchi Art Triennale takes place here and on the surrounding islands, showcasing new permanent and temporary art installations over the years—a perfect excuse to visit more than once in a lifetime.

A favorite architectural moment/scene in cinema? The dystopian urban landscapes of *Blade Runner* set the perfect scenography for a critical view of our possible future. In this scenario, projects from different ages are recontextualized to feel part of this futuristic, dark atmosphere moving between the Bradbury Building by George Wyman and Sumner Hunt (1893) and Frank Lloyd Wright's Ennis House (1924).

Do you have a favorite quote about architecture? My favorite quote is a popular expression, used by Rafael Moneo in his Prince of Asturias Award acceptance speech in 2012. It evokes the evolution of architecture, which over centuries has become a highly specialized profession, but which, in its primitive nature, is still of importance to all of society: "There is an architect inside every one of us."

What's your favorite architect/artist collaboration? The work of Snarkitecture, a collaboration between American artist Daniel Arsham and architect Alex Mustonen. It's the perfect example of how art and architecture can nourish and push one another, creating works where the blurred boundaries of each discipline meet to encompass structures, atmospheres, experiences, and unique material research.

The island of Naoshima, an art and architecture experience in Japan.

Agustina Coulleri
PROJECTS CURATOR

Recommend a lesser-known urban architectural gem. Sperlonga in Italy, a seaside town south of Rome. It was built as if it were a single colossal house—you are unable to tell where one house begins and the next ends. The constructions feature the characteristic white walls of the Mediterranean style, while the town's narrow streets barely allow a small group of people to pass. The stairs lead from one street to the next and, if you are lucky, you will find the main square of the town next to its beautiful church.

Sperlonga, a hidden gem halfway between Rome and Naples.

What's your all-time favorite museum? The one that has not been built yet. Museums are evolving more rapidly than ever, and, at some point, they are going to appear as exhibitions in themselves because of the statement they make. However, there are some interesting open-air museums that are already redefining the way we exhibit art, such as the Chillida Leku in Spain.

What's the world's most beautiful building? The Pantheon in Rome. Not only because its dome was—and remains—a masterpiece of engineering, but also because of its use of lighting. We have to recall that it is a grave and the lights are there to thrill.

At 43 m (141 ft), the Pantheon's span was the largest of any dome until the 20th century.

What's your favorite architect/artist collaboration? My favorite collaboration was between Lina Bo Bardi and popular folk artists of the Brazilian northeast for a 1963 show at the Modern Art Museum of Bahía, dubbed "Civilização do Nordeste." When everyone else was looking towards developed civilizations, Bo Bardi was able to find great inspiration and beauty in folk art. She knew how to combine its ideas with those of modern architecture, and understood it could be preserved through exhibition in a museum.

Hana Abdel Latif
PROJECTS CURATOR

If you could live in any building, where would you choose? My personal living requirements and tastes tend to shift, calling for different types of spaces. Therefore, one of the most architecturally appealing houses to me—particularly in its layout and interior styling—is the Maison de Verre by Bernard Bijvoet and Pierre Chareau. This glass-fronted house is an experimental project that cannot be seen from the main street, but can be marveled at from the back courtyard as its translucent glass-block facade is illuminated. This offers soft natural light to the open and versatile interior space. The house, which doubled as the client's residence and medical clinic, contains multiple mechanisms that offer flexible and adaptable modes of living. These materials lend to the attractive industrial look of the house.

What's your architectural pet peeve? There are quite a few *faux-pas* to be found in some architectural works. However, one that is particularly offputting is when an architecturally interesting project or layout is obstructed by excessive or distasteful ornamentation, whether exterior or interior. Though it might be reflective of the client's personal taste, it can easily and unknowingly become overwhelming along with other day-to-day furnishings, supplies, and accessories, thus making an initially well-conceived work appear messy.

Name the building/s that made you fall in love with architecture. My love of architecture and understanding of its influence and language began early on, following a trip to Egypt and a fateful visit to the Temple of Hatshepsut in Luxor. It is a stirring architectural revelation and a mesmerizing exploration of the ancient temple, which is still referenced in many modern and contemporary works today. With its imposing central ramp and flaking colonnades, the temple is a striking yet harmonious monument built into a valley. It remains astonishing to me how, even back then, it was conceived with attention to proportions and symmetry. This building always appealed to me as an ancient precursor to modernism with its continuous horizontal lines, highlighted by the large stone lintels and relative simplicity. To me, this house is an ideal play space, especially as I am always dreaming up different projects and experimenting with spaces and moods.

Maison de Verre, where industrial materials meet traditional home decor.

Fabián Dejtiar

MANAGING EDITOR
OF *ARCHDAILY* IN SPANISH

Who takes the best photographs of architecture? Photography is storytelling and there are few contemporary photographers who know how to tell stories as well as Juan Alberto Andrade and Cuqui Rodríguez, founders of JAG Studio. Some of my favorite photos are the ones taken at El Guardián del Chimborazo (The Guardian of Chimborazo Shelter) in Ecuador, where snow and white clouds blend together. Moreover, their level of commitment to capturing the "essence" of a project goes beyond getting along with the architects. In a 2019 interview with *ArchDaily*, they noted that "the work of the architectural photographer has more and more … relevance [even as part of the projects themselves]," explaining that good imagery has now become a key part of a project itself.

Recommend a lesser-known urban architectural gem. The new City Hall of Nancagua in Chile by Beals Lyon really caught my attention in terms of bringing quality public architecture to a remote site. The project sets a remarkable public space within a small country town while committing to enhancing the value of local heritage.

Who's an architect everyone should know about? There are several contemporary exponents in Latin American architecture that deserve our attention: Gabriela Carrillo in Mexico, José Cubilla in Paraguay, and Daniel Flores in Ecuador, to name a few. But I find it even more interesting to look at other regions of the world to get inspired by similar practices and architects, such as Xu Tiantian from DnA office in China. I admire her interdisciplinary practice and design process based on research and discussion, which she has applied to a diverse array of projects, ranging from the Bamboo Theater to the Shimen Bridge.

History-imbued walls and architectural details shape Sala Beckett in Spain.

Which architectural detail matters to you most? Every detail has the potential to be important, as long as it is made so. I have seen architects putting all of their effort into the design of railings or gutters that have ultimately turned out to be one of the most outstanding parts of their buildings. For me, the most pertinent thing is when architectural details have historic links. Carrying out thorough research to discover them can lead to magnificent results, as evidenced in the work of Flores & Prats, such as the Casal Balaguer Cultural Center or Sala Beckett in Spain.

Mónica Arellano

EDITOR

What's your all-time favorite museum? The Jumex Museum by David Chipperfield in Mexico City. My favorite space is the multifunctional hall that connects with the main circulation nucleus and extends towards the outdoor esplanade, which in turn connects to the restaurant, making it a visually and spatially fluid place. The building orientation responds to the architects' interest in maintaining adequate circulation and its form evokes the historic industrial background of the plot.

A favorite architectural moment/scene in cinema. One of my favorite moments is a scene in *Roma*, a movie by Mexican filmmaker Alfonso Cuarón. Here, a specific moment in the history of Mexico City is captured in a tracking shot when the main character goes to the Las Américas cinema. This scene evokes the atmosphere of the city as it was in the 1970s, before it was dramatically transformed and reinvented in the search for that modern promise of progress that never came true. In addition to the visuals, the film sonically captures the energy of the streets, to truly immersive effect. Hands down, *Roma* remains a benchmark encapsulation of Mexico City as it was in the 20th century.

Do you have a favorite quote about architecture? Beatriz Colomina wrote in *Domesticity at War*: "The history of architecture is not simply the history of a building but also the history of what we think about them: the theories we build about them, the photographs we take of them, the conversations they provoke. Good institutions (publications, museums, schools, etc.) are those that not only record those conversations or teach established principles, but rather stimulate new conversations. Good architecture is always a provocation."

Name a building that stirs up intense emotions for you. When I was a student, the Capuchin Convent Chapel was one of the first buildings designed by Luis Barragán that I had the chance to visit. Despite being set amid the chaos of Mexico City, the silence that engulfs the main nave of the chapel as you enter plunges you into a state of meditation. Light and colors connect with specific times of the day and year, transforming the building into a contemplative place that invites us to look inside and question our place in the world.

Jumex Museum,
a freestanding pavilion
in Mexico City.

Victor Delaqua

COMMUNITY & SOCIAL MEDIA EDITOR

Name a building that stirs up intense emotions for you. The Faculty of Architecture and Urbanism of the University of São Paulo can move any architect. Here, Vilanova Artigas materializes his theory, language, and experimentations and makes the building a true "professor" of architecture. After all, its spatial generosity expands the possibilities of meeting and coexistence, sheltering students, professors, and citizens in the most different events—from parties to manifestations—demonstrating that a public building can lead to important collective debates that go beyond its program and become part of history.

Which space has the best interior design? At Casa da Música in Porto, Portugal, you come to understand how powerful the interior of a building can be, matching or superseding any iconic exterior. Through exquisite details and a rigorous choice of materials and textures, OMA demonstrates that it is possible to create a design that is at once contemporary, historical, and timeless, awakening the most distinct sensations in its inhabitants as they experience its beauty.

What's your favorite architect/artist collaboration? The Steilneset Memorial in Vardø, Norway, designed by Swiss architect Peter Zumthor and French-American artist Louise Bourgeois. Here, they merge their personal responses to the execution of 91 people for witchcraft in 1621 and translate them into a spatial intervention that—through the choice of materials and elements presented—enables a poetic connection with the past. It awakens myriad feelings that invite interpretation and self-reflection, ranging from historical fascination to deep empathy for the victims.

Name a building that evokes a special memory for you. After visiting any Lina Bo Bardi project, you will have the most special memories. Teatro Oficina in São Paulo is one such work. Bardi's design enhances "Brazilianness" above all other forms of theater, turning the space into a passageway or street that connects the theater to the city beyond. Inside, you find a tree growing, reaching towards the sky, an indoor water fountain, and a retractable roof that invites the stars inside—all elements of nature merging with the process of human artistic creation. This is an honest space that opens up theatrical performance to the most distinct of emotions.

Steilneset Memorial vividly embodies brutality, life, and emotions.

Shuang Han

MANAGING EDITOR
OF *ARCHDAILY* CHINA

Who takes the best photographs of architecture? Architectural photography is never a simple reproduction of architecture, but an interpretation based on understanding, transforming the depiction of an object into a valuable image. In photographs taken by Swiss-French architectural photographer Hélène Binet—especially of the walls of Suzhou Gardens, China—I see how she repeatedly captures the dialogue between line, light, shadow, white space, close-up and background, object, composition, and texture to form a narrative of independent autonomy.

Recommend a lesser-known urban architectural gem. Huang Sheng-Yuan's Fieldoffice Architects team has been building in Yilan, Taiwan, for over 20 years. His architecture does not have a grand narrative or exaggerated shapes; it is work that must be felt from the inside. His architectural philosophy is that "architecture is a kind of companionship." And of his many interpretations of "inclusion," the one that most touches me is the inclusion of ugliness, mediocrity, disadvantage, and a lack of excitement. The collision and disorder in daily materials—and in life itself—are the essential problems that architecture needs to face.

Which building do you consider architecturally perfect? Peter Zumthor's Shelter for Roman Ruins is the building that has struck me the most. A lightweight, wood-made wall frame that accommodates light and ventilation, precisely follows the construction rules assigned to ancient Roman facades and gives the building a weight that is distinguishable to the naked eye in contemporary cities. I feel the relative passage of time as I stroll through the delicate pergola wrapped around the rough earth. The construction, the details, and the architecture itself are just right.

Huang Sheng-Yuan's Fieldoffice Architects has been building in Yilan, Taiwan, for over 20 years.

Which architectural detail matters to you most? I have a serious obsession with architectural details, I care a lot about the design of each node, and the rigor of construction. I will look at all the modular skins to see if they are aligned and if all the calculations are reasonable. Moreover, if they are rough, then they should have been deliberately designed so by the architect.

Diego Hernández

CREATIVE DIRECTOR

Which building do you consider architecturally perfect? There are few buildings that can achieve perfection, but there is one that made me fall in love with architecture again: The Salk Institute by Louis Kahn. This building reflects everything that a perfect structure should have, from habitability to details, materials, and a relationship with its context. The view from the central patio over the horizon is part of the memorabilia of every architect.

Who takes the best photographs of architecture? I find the documentation process of Erieta Attali and Laurian Ghinitoiu very interesting. Both photographers manage to show structures from a global perspective and, at the same time, capture everything that surrounds them. Thanks to them, I managed to understand how a building should be seen in a general way, before going into detail.

Which restaurant has the most inspiring architecture? The architectural experience in a restaurant has to be holistic, like Smiljan Radic's Mestizo Restaurant: a building without walls where art cannot be hung. The reinforced concrete beams, supported by massive granite slabs from the Andes, cannot fail to impress, while the brutalist expression is reflected in the Mapuche-inspired cuisine, resulting in a space that completes the experience of food and architecture.

Who's an architect everyone should know about? There is a Chilean architect who does not have the international recognition that he should have. Fernando Castillo Velasco was one of those architects who did everything in life. He was even a politician—something that every architect should be, in spirit at least—and a rector at one of the best universities in the country. Moreover, he managed to give quality and dignity to housing projects with humble materials in an unmatched way.

With its monastery-inspired layout, the Salk Institute is a secluded intellectual hub.

Kahn envisioned a bright and welcoming structure, quite unlike other institutional buildings.

Valeria Montjoy

BRANDS & MATERIALS EDITOR

What's your architectural pet peeve? When buildings overuse glass as a symbol of progress and contemporary aesthetics, often disregarding comfort, privacy, and—above all—sustainability. I especially object to curtain walls that do not incorporate shading solutions, leading to higher energy consumption and carbon emissions that we cannot afford to uphold. When you think about it, these are greenhouses being built during a climate crisis, which is quite problematic, to say the least—especially when we have access to the necessary knowledge, materials, and technologies to build sustainably.

Which architectural detail matters to you most? How materials join and fit together. In fact, how materials adjoin can be more impactful than the materials themselves. Although these connections tend to be hidden behind aesthetic-focused finishes, their importance lies in their ability to define the structural and functional quality of a building. Ultimately, well-assembled cheap materials will most likely achieve better results than badly joined expensive materials.

Name a building that stirs up intense emotions for you. The experience I had in Gaudí's Sagrada Familia is something that I will never forget. Both looking at it from afar within the Barcelona skyline and staring closely at its facade was amazing, but walking inside truly felt like a surreal and spiritual experience. With its fascinating use of light, bright colors, and impressive height, the basilica made me feel pure joy and awe. It was almost hard to believe that something so beautiful could exist.

Name a building that evokes a special memory for you. When I was young, I visited the Sydney Opera House.

Sagrada Familia, a masterpiece of Catalan modernism.

I vividly remember walking around and hearing about its unique design, engineering achievements, and technological innovations. In particular, I was very impressed by the Concert Hall, a majestic space with a high-vaulted ceiling and timber interior that contrasts with the heavy concrete shells. Besides being one of the first memories I have of living in Australia, the experience motivated me to study architecture later on in life.

Paula Pintos

PROJECTS CURATOR

Which far-flung building would you plan a vacation around? While researching the Austrian architect Carl Pruscha, I discovered his work in Nepal, which I was not very familiar with. Pruscha combines Nepalese vernacular building techniques with a modern architectural approach. Out of all of his projects there, I would love to visit the Taragaon Museum, a beautiful, modern barrel-vaulted complex of brick and glass structures with strong references to Kathmandu's indigenous architecture of traditional Buddhist monastic cells. After a visit to the museum and the Nepalese capital, the perfect plan would be a trip to the astonishing Great Himalayan Trail.

What's your all-time favorite museum? One of my favorite museums is SANAA's New Museum in Manhattan. The scale of this museum allows visitors to walk through the gallery's collections at an easier pace. In this sense, as well as the way in which the building is inserted into the neighborhood's urban fabric, the New Museum is perfect. The stacked up and shifted volumes, together with its metallic mesh facade, create a playful and dynamic yet light composition that is recognizable both from the exterior and interiors, creating a great route for the visitor from the Lower East Side's streets into the galleries.

Which architectural detail matters to you most? I really value when constructive details are thoroughly thought out and resolved, and are coherent with the entire concept of the project. One of the things I appreciate the most is when the materials used are being applied and treated to exploit their natural properties and potential.

Name the building/s that made you fall in love with architecture. The building that assured me I love architecture was Álvaro Siza Vieira's Portuguese Pavilion in Lisbon. In my first year in architecture school, I had to build a model of it, and while it was a challenge to recreate a curved concrete slab of that scale, I was just amazed that something like that could be done so perfectly. I later had the opportunity to visit it and experience the public plaza space created by an incredibly thin concrete canopy hanging so gracefully between the porticoes.

New Museum: a simple, clear, strong composition in New York's Manhattan.

Danae Santibáñez

COMMUNITY &
SOCIAL MEDIA MANAGER

A favorite architectural moment/scene in cinema? I truly enjoy Italian film director Dario Argento's work. Considering he specializes in thriller movies, I find it particularly interesting how he chooses his unique settings and plays with different perspectives. The opening of his 1975 film *Profondo Rosso* is just outstanding: the iconic, red-velvet theater interior and the game of different perspectives that Argento utilizes to create suspense are wonderful.

What's your all-time favorite museum? Every now and then I switch my favorite museum—it definitely depends on my mood and what I am looking for. However, I have always enjoyed smaller museums rather than massive ones, because I like to have the opportunity to visit the entire collection. For a long time, I was compelled by the Tamayo Museum in Mexico City, designed by Abraham Zabludovsky and Teodoro González de León. Nowadays I quite enjoy the Musée de l'Orangerie in Paris: I like the diverse history of the site, how it was developed by different architects, and how it is the perfect size and design to hold Monet's *Water Lilies*.

Tamayo Museum: a bold array of interior spaces suffused with natural light.

What's your favorite architect/artist collaboration? I love when architecture and art mix well together. That is why I want to highlight a place that I recently visited, the Trinity Laban Conservatoire of Music and Dance in London. This Herzog & de Meuron project exhibits a collaboration with the visual artist Michael Craig-Martin. The color-intervened translucent facade creates a calm and peaceful atmosphere—the ideal break from one's daily routine. On a sunny day, the colorful reflections complement the artificial-grass landscape, providing a perfect spot to rest.

Trinity Laban Conservatoire, where art, dance, and architecture meet in London.

Eduardo Leite Souza

BRANDS & MATERIALS EDITOR

If you could live in any building, where would you choose? I would choose to live in the Eames House, by Charles and Ray Eames, or in any of the Case Study Houses on the outskirts of Los Angeles in the 1950s. Even though it was built under the aegis of efficiency and resource-saving, Eames House is extremely cozy, featuring natural light and abundant ventilation, while inspiring creativity in each of its technical solutions, colors, and material choices.

What's your architectural pet peeve? I really feel reluctant about materials that try to imitate others: ceramics that mimic stones, panels that imitate wood, and concrete-colored tiles. It seems somewhat curious that the industry spends so much energy trying to recreate imperfections and small variations that are characteristic of natural materials.

Who's an architect everyone should know about? João Filgueiras Lima, also known as "Lelé." He had a very comprehensive career, developing several prefabricated solutions when the world knew very little about them. Lelé designed various scales and programs, from homes to churches; developed hospitals that allowed natural ventilation, under the precepts of bioclimatic architecture. He was able to achieve extremely pleasant spaces thermally speaking, where the quality of the air exceeds the standard of buildings that currently have very expensive climate control.

Name a building that evokes a special memory for you. The Jewish Museum Berlin by Daniel Libeskind. Even though I am not Jewish, and have only known the horrors of the Holocaust through movies and books, the building was able to profoundly transmit this terrible episode of humanity to me.

The Case Study Houses program was an American residential architecture experiment.

The staircases without intermediate levels, the very narrow corridors, the coldness of the material palette, and many other details make it impossible to feel impassive about the museum's subject matter. This architecture gives us a sense of permanent discomfort, especially the last room on one of the museum's three routes, called the Holocaust Tower, which is completely dark, all concrete, and features just a small opening—it is uniquely touching.

Susanna Moreira

PROJECTS CURATOR

Recommend a lesser-known urban architectural gem. Ladeira da Misericórdia, in Salvador de Bahía, Brazil. It is one of the first communication points between the historical upper and lower parts of the city, and in the 1980s was subject to an intervention by Lina Bo Bardi in collaboration with João Filgueiras Lima. The project saw the development of three houses and a ruin into social housing, and a vacant lot into a restaurant, using a system of prefabricated concrete structural components. It combines—in an experimental and inventive way—modernist and vernacular design approaches, resulting in an intriguing dialogue between contemporaneity and tradition. Unfortunately, despite being a public street, it is usually closed to the public and can only be accessed when artistic interventions happen.

What's your all-time favorite museum? It is difficult to choose just one, but I would pick the Centre Pompidou in Paris. Besides its boldness and timeless innovation, which surprised when it was unveiled in 1971, and continues to do so today, it exceeded all the expectations I had as a university student when I visited it for the first time—and then again the second time a few years ago.

Name the building/s that made you fall in love with architecture. The first time I went to São Paulo for college entrance exams I was not sure which course to study, but the Centro Cultural São Paulo (CCSP) was one of the buildings that helped me make up my mind. It was an Architecture Biennial year and the CCSP was one of the exhibition points. The building, the exhibition, and the city itself seemed strongly connected with each other, interwoven with the urban dynamics of São Paulo. My perception was strengthened by how freely people interacted with a building that promoted different uses of the space.

What's your favorite architect/artist collaboration? Among the many collaborations between architects and artists in modern Brazilian architecture—particularly in regards to the use of tiled panels—one of my favorites is the Pampulha Church in Belo Horizonte. As a significant example of Oscar Niemeyer's embrace of Portinari's iconic tiles, this building really stands out, with its concrete vaults in different sizes that act as an unpretentious frame highlighting the white and blue pictorial panel made up of tiles.

Pampulha Church: an experiment in striking curved forms.

FOOTNOTES

How Can You Build a Community? (pp. 130-133)

1. Harrouk, Christele, "Hashim Sarkis: 'I Do Not Think We Have Ever Witnessed a Moment Where We Have Relied as Much on Architecture,'" ArchDaily, 2020.
2. Harrouk, Christele, "'Cultural Identity is Central to Architecture': In Conversation with Lesley Lokko," ArchDaily, 2021.
3. Valencia, Nicolás, "Carlos García Vázquez: 'The Modern Urbanism Has Rediscovered Traditional Cities,'" ArchDaily, 2020.
4. Harrouk, C., "Cultural Identity is Central to Architecture."
5. Tamas, Andrea, "Interview: Robert Venturi & Denise Scott Brown, by Andrea Tamas," ArchDaily, 2011.

Materials Stimulating Good Architecture (pp. 150-153)

1. Frangoul, Anmar, "Building Materials Powerhouse LafargeHolcim Launches Its 'Green Concrete' in the U.S.," CNBC, July 24, 2020.
2. "ECOPact, The Green Concrete," Holcim, 2020.
3. "Cemfree," DB Group, 2019.
4. Franco, José Tomás, "Is Cross-Laminated Timber (CLT) the Concrete of the Future?" ArchDaily, 2019.
5. The International Building Code (IBC), "Overview of the International Building Code® (IBC®)", 2018.
6. Montjoy, Valeria, "Can 3D Printing Reshape Residential Architecture as We Know It?" ArchDaily, 2022.
7. Souza, Eduardo, "Is It Possible to Mix Local Materials and 3D Printing?" ArchDaily, 2021.
8. "2021 Global Status Report for Buildings and Construction," Global Alliance for Buildings and Construction, 2021.
9. Emmons, Paul, "Drawing Imagining Building: Embodiment in Architectural Design Practices," Routledge, 2019.

Identity: A Result, Not a Starting Point (pp. 194-197)

1. Baratto, Romullo, "It's Not Because You Are Limited in Resources That You Should Accept Mediocrity," Interview with Francis Kéré, 2022 Pritzker Winner", ArchDaily, 2022
2. Venezuela, Colombia, Ecuador, and Costa Rica are among the countries where this type of collective—working directly in impoverished districts (by themselves, or either academic or government support)—has emerged.
3. Montaner, Josep Maria, "La condición contemporánea de la arquitectura," Gustavo Gili, 2015.
4. Durán Calisto, Ana María, "Arquitectura contemporánea de Ecuador (1999-2015): El florecimiento de una crisis," Rita, 2015.
5. Snyder, Michael, "In Chile, Homes as Extreme as the Landscape Itself," The New York Times, March 19, 2019.
6. Baratto, R.

Back to the Future: Why Refurbishing Matters (pp. 252-255)

1. "2021 Global Status Report for Buildings and Construction," Global Alliance for Buildings and Construction (GlobalABC), 2021.
2. "Sixth Assessment Report (AR6)," Intergovernmental Panel on Climate Change, 2022.
3. "State of the Climate in Latin America and the Caribbean 2020," World Meteorological Organization, 2021; "State of the Climate in Africa 2020," United Nations Commission for Africa, 2021, and "State of the Climate in Asia 2020," World Meteorological Organization, 2021.
4. Baratto, Romullo, "'It's Not Because You Are Limited in Resources That You Should Accept Mediocrity': Interview with Francis Kéré, 2022 Pritzker Winner," ArchDaily, 2022.
5. Hillebrandt, Annette; Riegler-Floors, Petra; Rosen, Anja; Seggewies, Johanna, "Manual of Recycling: Buildings as Sources of Materials," Detail, 2019.

Solutions for Living Better, Together (pp. 282-285)

1. Paulin, Geoffrey, "Fun facts about Millennials: Comparing Expenditure Patterns from the Latest through the Greatest Generation," U.S. Bureau of Labor Statistics, 2018.
2. Parker, Kim and Horowitz, Juliana Menasce, "Majority of workers who quit a job in 2021 cite low pay, no opportunities for advancement, feeling disrespected," Pew Research Center, 2022.

23 SUL
23SUL.COM.BR

Administrative Headquarters of the Mosaic of Juréia-Itatins Conservation Units
pp. 242–245
Photography: Pedro Kok / pedrokok.com
Responsible Architect: Mario do Val
Project Team: Lucas Menezes, Chayenne Cardoso, Priscila Fernandes

ABIN DESIGN STUDIO
ABINDESIGNSTUDIO.COM

Gallery House
pp. 122–125
Photography: Courtesy of Abin Design Studio / Edmund Sumner / edmundsumner.co.uk

ADJAYE ASSOCIATES
ADJAYE.COM

Ruby City Contemporary Art Center
pp. 126–129
Photography: Mark Menjivar (pp.127–128, 129 top and bottom left), Dror Baldinger (p. 129 bottom right)

AKIHISA HIRATA ARCHITECTURE OFFICE
HAO.NU

Tree-ness House
pp. 300–303
Photography: Vincent Hecht / a-vh.com
Principal Architect: Akihisa Hirata
Project Architect: Yuko Tonogi
Design Team: Oba Kohei, Masatoshi Sugiyama
Planting Designer: Yuichi Tsukada (Onshitsu)
Textile Designer: Yoko Ando, Kasumi Yamaguchi (Yoko Ando Design)

ALBOR ARQUITECTOS
ALBORARQUITECTOS.COM

Casa Torre
pp. 58–61, 282 bottom
Photography: Albor Arquitectos
Albor Members: Carlos Manuel González Baute, Alain Rodríguez Sosa, Camilo José Cabrera Pérez, Merlyn González García

ATELIER FCJZ
FCJZ.COM

Jishou Art Museum
pp. 12–13, 292–295
Photography: Tian Fangfang

ATELIER XI
ATELIERXI.COM

Peach Hut Community Center
pp. 34–37, 132 top right
Photography: Courtesy of Atelier Xi / Zhang Chao
Lead Architect: Chen Xi
Design Team: Zhu Zhu, Huang Jiajie, Wang Xingyao, Xu Lvbao, Wang Weiguo, Tian Di, Wen Weijian, Cao Suying, Han Xiao, Xu Zhiwei

ATELIERS JEAN NOUVEL
JEANNOUVEL.COM

Henderson Cifi Tiandi
pp. 312–315
Photography: Courtesy of Ateliers Jean Nouvel / © 10 Studio
© Jean Nouvel / VG Bild-Kunst, Bonn 2022

AVANTO ARCHITECTS
AVAN.TO

Löyly Public Sauna
pp. 168–171
Photography: Courtesy of Avanto Architects / Anders Portman / kuvio.com
Kyrö Barrell Stage Building
pp. 210–211
Photography: Courtesy of Avanto Architects / Anders Portman / kuvio.com
Lead Architects: Ville Hara, Anu Puustinen

BAK GORDON ARQUITECTOS
BAKGORDON.COM

House in Grândola
pp. 98–102
Photography: Courtesy of Bak Gordon Arquitectos / Francisco Nogueira / francisconogueira.com

BANGKOK PROJECT STUDIO
BANGKOKPROJECTSTUDIO.CO

Elephant World Cultural Courtyard
pp. 118–121
Photography: Courtesy of Bangkok Project Studio / Spaceshift Studio / spaceshiftstudio.com

BARCLAY & CROUSSE ARCHITECTURE
BARCLAYCROUSSE.COM

Place of Remembrance
p. 133 top right
Photography: Cristobal Palma / estudiopalma.cl

BETA OFFICE FOR ARCHITECTURE AND THE CITY
BETA-OFFICE.COM

Three Generation House
pp. 283, 286–289
Photography: Courtesy of BETA / Ossip van Duivenbode

BIG - BJARKE INGELS GROUP
BIG.DK

Superkilen
p. 131
Photography: Iwan Baan / iwan.com
Partners-in-Charge: Bjarke Ingels
Project Leaders: Nanna Gyldholm Møller, Mikkel Marcker Stubgaard
CopenHill
pp. 238–241
Photography: Courtesy of BIG / Rasmus Hjortshøj / coastarc.com (pp. 238–239, 241) & Soren Aagaard / sorenaagaard.dk (p. 240 top)
Partners-in-Charge: Bjarke Ingels, David Zahle, Jakob Lange, Brian Yang
Project Leaders: Jesper Boye Andersen, Claus Hermansen, Nanna Gyldholm Møller

BLOCK RESEARCH GROUP, ETH ZURICH
BLOCK.ARCH.ETHZ.CH

Armadillo Vault
p. 150 bottom
Photography: Iwan Baan / iwan.com
Block Research Group, ETH Zurich; Ochsendorf DeJong & Block (ODB Engineering); Escobedo Group
NEST HiLo
pp. 151–152
Photography: Courtesy of ETH Zurich / Juney-Lee (p. 151 top right & middle right), courtesy of ETH Zurich / Naida Iljazovic (p. 152 bottom left)
Block Research Group, ETH Zurich; Architecture and Building Systems Group, ETH Zurich Architecture; ROK Architects
Striatus
p. 151 bottom & middle left
Photography: Courtesy of ETH Zurich / naaro & In3D
ETH Zurich - Block Research Group, ETH Zurich (BRG); Zaha Hadid Architects - Computation and Design Group (ZHACODE); in collaboration with incremental3D, made possible by Holcim
KnitCandela
p. 153
Photography: Courtesy of ETH Zurich / Maria Verhulst (p. 153 middle left), Courtesy of ETH Zurich / Lex Reiter (p. 153 bottom left), Courtesy of ETH Zurich / Mariana_Popescu (p. 153 top & bottom right);
Block Research Group, ETH Zurich (BRG); Zaha Hadid Architects Computation and Design Group (ZHCODE); Architecture Extrapolated (R-Ex)

CCA CENTRO DE COLABORACIÓN ARQUITECTÓNICA
CCA.MX

Club de Niños y Niñas
pp. 114–117
Photography: Courtesy of CCA Centro de Colaboración Arquitectónica / Arturo Arrieta (pp.115–116), Jaime Navarro (pp. 117 top & bottom left) & Onnis Luque (p. 117 bottom right)

CHANG ARCHITECTS
CHANGARCH.COM

Cornwall Gardens House
pp. 296–299
Photography: Courtesy of CHANG Architects

COBE
COBE.DK

Israels Plads
pp. 104–107, 132 middle right
Photography: Courtesy of Cobe / Rasmus Hjortshøj / coastarc.com
The Silo
pp. 230–233, 252
Photography: Courtesy of Cobe / Rasmus Hjortshøj / coastarc.com

DANIEL MORENO + SEBASTIAN CALERO

Casa en el Carrizal
p. 197
Photography: Courtesy of Daniel Moreno + Sebastian Calero / Lorena Darquea (p. 197 top) & Andres Villota Pelusa (197 bottom)

DANIELA BUCIO SISTOS
INSTAGRAM.COM/DANIELABSISTOS

Casa UC
pp. 94–97
Photography: Dane Alonso / danealonso.com
Lead Architect: Daniela Bucio Sistos
Construction: Daniela Bucio Sistos, Edel Hernández
Other Participants: Isabel Molina Plaza, Edel Hernandez, Gonzalo Nares, Luisa Sistos Mier

DAVID CHIPPERFIELD ARCHITECTS
DAVIDCHIPPERFIELD.COM

James-Simon-Galerie
pp. 40–43
Photography: Simon Menges / simonmenges.com (pp. 40–41, 43 top) & Ute Zscharnt for David Chipperfield Architects (pp.42, 43 bottom)
Architect: David Chipperfield Architects Berlin
Partners: David Chipperfield, Martin Reichert, Alexander Schwarz (Design lead) Project architect Urs Vogt (Preparation and brief to Technical design, Site design supervision)
Neue Nationalgalerie
pp. 234–237, 253 (top & middle right)
Photography: Simon Menges / simonmenges.com
Architect: David Chipperfield Architects Berlin
Partners: David Chipperfield, Martin Reichert, Alexander Schwarz
Project Architects: Daniel Wendler and Michael Freytag
©VG Bild-Kunst, Bonn 2022 for the work of Mies van der Rohe

DORTE MANDRUP
DORTEMANDRUP.DK

Community Centre Herstedlund
p. 130
Photography: Courtesy of Dorte Mandrup / Adam Mørk

EL EQUIPO DE MAZZANTI
ELEQUIPOMAZZANTI.COM

Fundación Santa Fe de Bogotá
pp. 54–57
Photography: Courtesy of El Equipo de Mazzanti / Alejandro Arango
Team Members:
Principal Arch. Giancarlo Mazzanti,
Arch. Sebastián Negret,
Arch. Fredy Fortich,
Arch. Alberto Aranda,
Arch. Felipe Pombo,
Arch. Rocío Lamprea

ELEMENTAL
ELEMENTALCHILE.CL

Portrait Image: p. 274
Photography: getty images / Awakening / Contributor
Quinta Monroy
pp. 28–29
Photography: Cristobal Palma / estudiopalma.cl (p. 28), Courtesy of ELEMENTAL / Tadeuz Jalocha (p. 29)
Centro de Innovación UC
pp. 275, 277 (top)
Photography: Cristobal Palma / estudiopalma.cl
Zocalo Turisticao
p. 276
Photography: Cristobal Palma / estudiopalma.cl
Colegio San Juan
p. 277 (bottom)
Photography: Cristobal Palma / estudiopalma.cl
Colegio Ayelen
pp. 278–279
Photography: Cristobal Palma / estudiopalma.cl
Aguas Claras
pp. 280 (top), 281
Photography: Cristobal Palma / estudiopalma.cl
Poligono Illapel
p. 280 (bottom)
Photography: Cristobal Palma / estudiopalma.cl

ENSAMBLE
ENSAMBLE.INFO

Ca'n Terra
pp. 136–141
Photography: Iwan Baan / iwan.com (pp. 136–138, 139 top, 140–141), ENSAMBLE (p. 139 bottom)
Author of the project: Antón García-Abril & Debora Mesa Molina

HEATHERWICK STUDIO
HEATHERWICK.COM

Maggie's Yorkshire
pp. 20–23
Photography: Hufton & Crow / huftonandcrow.com

HERZOG & DE MEURON
HERZOGDEMEURON.COM

1111 Lincoln Road
pp. 258–261
Photography: Hufton and Crow / huftonandcrow.com (pp. 259–260, 261 bottom), Iwan Baan / iwan.com (p. 261 top)

HOLCIM
HOLCIM.DE

Seattle Spheres
p. 150 top
Photography: Courtesy of Holcim / Sean Airhart / nbbj.com

HOPKINS ARCHITECTS
HOPKINS.CO.UK

Khor Kalba Turtle and Wildlife Sanctuary
pp. 220–223
Photography: Courtesy of Hopkins Architects / Marc Goodwin / archmospheres.com

Principal and Lead-Designer: Simon Fraser
Director: Andrew Ardill
Project Director: Tim Sheridan
Project Architect: Angus McDougall

IBUKU
IBUKU.COM

The Arc at Green School
pp. 146–149
Photography: Tommaso Riva / tommasoriva.com
Concept: Jörg Stamm
Engineering: Atelier One
Construction: Bamboo Pure
For evening photographs
Lighting: Studio Nimmersatt @studio_nimmersatt

ISAY WEINFELD
ISAYWEINFELD.COM

Paula Raia Boutique and Atelier
pp. 262–265
Photography: Courtesy of Isay Weinfeld / Fernando Guerra
360° Building
p. 305
Photography: Courtesy of Isay Weinfeld / Fernando Guerra
AB Apartment
p. 306
Photography: Courtesy of Isay Weinfeld / Fernando Guerra
Grecia House
p. 307 top
Photography: Courtesy of Isay Weinfeld / Fernando Guerra
Fazenda Boa Vista
p. 307 bottom
Photography: Courtesy of Isay Weinfeld / Fernando Guerra
Oito Building
p. 308 bottom
Photography: Courtesy of Isay Weinfeld / Fernando Guerra
Fasano Las Piedras
p. 309, 310 top
Photography: Courtesy of Isay Weinfeld / Fernando Guerra
Azul Building
p. 310 bottom
Photography: Courtesy of Isay Weinfeld / Fernando Guerra
Das Figueiras House
p. 311
Photography: Courtesy of Isay Weinfeld / Fernando Guerra

JAJA ARCHITECTS
JAJA.ARCHI

Park 'n' Play
pp. 30–33
Photography: Courtesy of JAJA Architects / Rasmus Hjortshøj / coastarc.com

K-STUDIO
K-STUDIO.GR

Dexamenes Seaside Hotel
pp. 226–229, 253 (bottom & middle left)
Photography: Claus Brechenmacher & Reiner Baumann / brechenmacher-baumann.com

KÉRÉ ARCHITECTURE
KEREARCHITECTURE.COM

Startup Lions Campus
Pp. 173, 180–181, 196 bottom left
Photography: Courtesy of Kéré Architecture / Kinan Deeb
TUM Tower
p. 174
Render: Courtesy of Kéré Architecture
National Assembly of Burkina Faso
p. 175
Renders: Courtesy of Kéré Architecture
Serpentine Pavilion
p. 176 bottom
Photography: Iwan Baan / iwan.com
Burkina Institute of Technology: BIT
p. 177
Photography: Courtesy of Kéré Architecture
The Center for Health and Social Advancement
p. 178 top, 179
Photography: Courtesy of Kéré Architecture
Sarbalé Ke
p. 178 bottom
Photography: Iwan Baan / iwan.com
National Park of Mali
p. 196 top right
Photography: Courtesy of Kéré Architecture
Gando Primary School
p. 196 middle right
Photography: Courtesy of Kéré Architecture / Erik-Jan Owerkerk
Lycée Schorge Secondary School
pp. 216–219
Photography: Iwan Baan / iwan.com (pp. 216, 218, 219 bottom), Courtesy of Kéré Architecture / Andrea Maretto (pp. 217, 219 top)

KIYOAKI TAKEDA ARCHITECTS
KIYOAKITAKEDA.COM

Tsuruoka House
pp. 108–111
Photography: Masaki hamada / kkpo.co.jp

LACOL
LACOL.COOP

La Borda
pp. 284–285
Photography: Courtesy of Lacol (pp. 284 bottom left & middle right, 285 top), Ivaro Valdecantos (pp. 284 top right, 285 bottom left) & Iluc Miralles (p. 285 bottom right)

MAD ARCHITECTS
I-MAD.COM

YueCheng Courtyard Kindergarten
pp. 316–319
Photography: Hufton and Crow / huftonandcrow.com (pp. 316 top, 319), Courtesy of MAD Architects / Tian Fangfang (p. 316 bottom) & Arch-Exist / arch-exist.com (pp. 317-318)
Chief Architect:
MAD Architects Executive
Architect: China Academy of Building Research
Interior Design: MAD Architects, Supercloud Studio
Landscape Architect: MAD Architects, ECOLAND Planning and Design Corporation

MARIO CUCINELLA ARCHITECTS + WASP
MCARCHITECTS.IT

STUDIOWASP.COM

TECLA House
pp. 144–145, 152 (top right & middle right)
Photography: Courtesy of Mario Cucinella Architects / Iago Corazza
Architectural and Furniture Project: Mario Cucinella Architects;
Team: Mario Cucinella (founder and creative director), Irene Giglio (project manager), Augusto Barichello
Sustainability Research: SOS – School of Sustainability, Bologna, Italy (Postgraduate Training Center founded by Mario Cucinella): Lorenzo Porcelli, Stefano Rosso, Lori Zillante
Collaborative 3D Printing Technology Project: WASP, Massa Lombarda, Ravenna, Italy;
Team: Massimo Moretti (Founder), Alberto Chiusoli, Francesco De Fabritiis, Lapo Naldoni, Massimo Visonà

MOHAMED AMINE SIANA
INSTAGRAM.COM/SIANAARCHITECTE

Villa Z
pp. 212–215
Photography: Courtesy of Mohamed Amine Siana / doublespace photography / doublespacephoto.com
Architect: Mohamed Amine Siana
Team: Yassine El Aouni, Rachid El Maataoui

NASO
NASO.MX

Casa Martha
pp. 204–207
Photography: Courtesy of Naso / Maureen M. Evans / maureenme.com / instagram.com/maureenme
Design Team: Patricio Aldrett, Julia Ruiz-Cabello, José Ignacio Vargas
Landscape Design: Aldaba
Furniture Design: Nomah

NATURA FUTURA ARQUITECTURA
NATURAFUTURARQ.COM

La Comuna
pp. 190–193
Photography: Natura Futura Arquitectura
The Provider Productive Center
p. 194
Photography: Courtesy of Natura Futura Arquitectura
La Pradería Sports Integration Center for Rural Areas
p. 195
Photography: Courtesy of Natura Futura Arquitectura

NIKKEN SEKKEI
NIKKEN.CO.JP

Miyashita Park
pp. 16–19, 132 bottom left
Photography: Courtesy of Nikken Sekkei / Nacása & Partners Inc. (pp. 17, 18, 19 bottom, 132 bottom left) & Shin Shasin Kobo (p. 19 top)
Architects: Takenaka Corporation + Nikken Sekkei Ltd
Lead Architect: Takenaka Corporation
Project Architect: Nikken Sekkei Ltd

OPEN ARCHITECTURE
OPENARCH.COM

Chapel of Sound
pp. 90–93
Photography: courtesy of OPEN Architecture / Jonathan Leijonhufvud
Architectural and Interior Design: OPEN Principals in Charge: LI Hu, HUANG Wenjing
Project Team: ZHOU Tingting, FANG Kuanyin, HUANG Zetian, LIN Bihong, JIA Han, CHEN Xiuyuan, CAI Zhuoqun, KUO Chunchen, TANG Ziqiao

PEZO VON ELLRICHSHAUSEN
PEZO.CL

INES Innovation Center
pp. 270–273
Photography: Pezo von Ellrichshausen

RO&AD ARCHITECTEN
RO-AD.ORG

Moses Bridge
pp. 142–143
Photography: RO&AD Architecten
Contributing Architects: Ro Koster, Ad Kil, Martin van Overveld

SANAA
SANAA.CO.JP

La Samaritaine
p. 255
Photography: Jared Chulski / jaredchulski.photography

SAUERBRUCH HUTTON
SAUERBRUCHHUTTON.DE

Haus 6
pp. 50–53, 282 top
Photography: Courtesy of Sauerbruch Hutton / © Jan Bitter / janbitter.de
Design Team: Louisa Hutton, Matthias Sauerbruch, Juan Lucas Young; Jürgen Bartenschlag, Vera Hartmann, Falco Herrmann, Amelie Hummel, Meta Popp, Karolina Sznajder; Quirin Dilling, Dianer Ding, Serafin Iannaccone, Abigail Yeadon

SEAN GODSELL ARCHITECTS
SEANGODSELL.COM

Shack in the Rocks
pp. 208–209
Photography: Courtesy of Sean Godsell Architects / Earl Carter / earlcarter.com.au

SELGASCANO
SELGASCANO.NET

Second Home Hollywood
pp. 86–89
Photography: Iwan Baan / iwan.com
Principals in Charge: José Selgas, Lucía Cano
Project Team: Diego Cano-Lasso, María Levene, Inés Olavarrieta, Paolo Tringali, Sixto Cordero, Víctor Jiménez, Sara Ouass, Pilar Cano-Lasso, Catalina Vázquez, Juan José Muñoz Muñoz, Julian Ocampo, Juan Saez Pedraja

SNØHETTA
SNOHETTA.COM

550 Madison Garden
p. 155
Render: Courtesy of Snøhetta
Calgary Public Library
pp. 156–157
Photography: Michael Grimm / mgrimm.com
Under
pp. 158–159, 162–165
Photography: Inger Marie Grini / ingermariegrini.no (pp. 158, 163, 165), shutterstock / Trygve Finkelsen (pp. 159, 164)
Theodore Roosevelt Presidential Library
p. 160
Renders: Courtesy of Snøhetta
Norwegian National Opera and Ballet
p. 161
Photography: Tasfoto / Alamy Stock Photo

STUDIO ANNE HOLTROP
ANNEHOLTROP.NL

35 Green Corner Building
pp. 72–75
Photography: Studio Anne Holtrop

STUDIO GANG
STUDIOGANG.COM

Aqua Tower
pp. 77, 79 bottom
Photography: Steve Hall / hallmerrick.com
Richard Gilder Center for Science, Education, and Innovation
pp. 78, 79 top
Renders: Courtesy of Studio Gang
WMS Boathouse at Clark Park
p. 80 bottom
Photography: Steve Hall / hallmerrick.com
Writers Theater
pp. 81, 82 top
Photography: Steve Hall / hallmerrick.com
Solar Carve 40 Tenth Avenue
p. 82 bottom
Photography: Courtesy of Studio Gang / Nic Lehoux / niclehoux.com
Nature Boardwalk At The Lincoln Park Zoo
p. 83
Photography: Steve Hall / hallmerrick.com
One Hundred
pp. 84–85
Photography: Matthew McFarland / mstudiowest.com
Studio Gang Design Team: Jeanne Gang, Mark Schendel, Juliane Wolf, Margaret Cavenagh, Aurelien Tsemo, Jason Flores, Melissa Long, John Dolci, Haoxiang Yang, William Emmick, Mauricio Sanchez, Magda Wala, Jay Hoffman, Harry Soenksen, Noora Aljabi, Franco Bolanos
Arcus Center for Social Justice Leadership
pp. 266–269
Photography: Steve Hall / hallmerrick.com (pp. 266, 267 top, 268 bottom, 269), Iwan Baan / iwan.com (pp. 267 bottom, 268 top)
Studio Gang Design Team: Jeanne Gang, Margaret Cavenagh, Claire Halpin, and Todd Zima, with John Castro, Juan de la Mora, Ana Maria Flor Ortiz, Wei-Ju Lai, Lindsey Moyer, Joana Ripple, Mark Schendel, Schuyler Smith, Rolf Temesvari, and John Wolters

STUDIO HOLLENSTEIN
STUDIOHOLLENSTEIN.COM

Green Square Library and Plaza
pp. 24–27, 133 bottom
Photography: Tom Roe/tomroephotography.com

STUDIO MK27
STUDIOMK27.COM.BR

Jungle House
pp. 68–71
Photography: Courtesy of Studio MK27/Fernando Guerra
Architect: Marcio Kogan
Co-architect: Samanta Cafardo
Interiors: Diana Radomysler
Project Team: Carlos Costa, Eline Ostyn, Laura Guedes, Mariana Ruzante, Mariana Simas, Oswaldo Pessano, Fernanda Neiva
Landscape Designer: Isabel Duprat
Structure Engineer: leão associados - eng. João rubens leão
Mep: grau engenharia
Air Conditioning: newest
Contractor: eng. Rogerio Biral

STUDIO OKAMI ARCHITECTEN
STUDIOOKAMI.COM

Riverside Tower
pp. 246–251, 254
Photography: Courtesy of Studio Okami Architecten/Olmo Peeters/olmopeeters.be (pp. 246–247, 249 top & bottom right, 254 middle right & bottom left), Tim Van de Velde/tvdv.be (pp. 248, 249 bottom left, 250 top, 254 top & bottom right), Studio Okami Architecten (pp. 250 bottom left & 251)

TRIPTYQUE
TRIPTYQUE.COM

Villa M
pp. 112–113
Photography: Courtesy of Triptyque/Michel Denancé (pp. 112, 113 bottom) & Triptyque (113 top)

VTN ARCHITECTS
VTNARCHITECTS.NET

Vedana Restaurant
pp. 186–189
Photography: Hiroyuki Oki
Principal Architect: Vo Trong Nghia
Design Team: Nguyen Tat Dat, Nguyen Duc Trung, Tu Minh Dong, Nguyen Tan Thang

WALLMAKERS
WALLMAKERS.ORG

Pirouette House
pp. 182–185
Photography: Courtesy of Wallmakers/Jino Sam
Design Team: Oshin Mariam Varughese, J.M.Srivarshini, Gayatri Maithani, Swathi Raj, Keerthi Kausalya, Shiuly Roy, Neeraj S. Murali, Dhawal Dasari

X ARCHITECTS
X-ARCHITECTS.COM

Wasit Wetland Center
pp. 200–203
Photography: Courtesy of X Architects/Fernando Guerra

XRANGE
XRANGE.NET

The Wandering Walls Bed and Breakfast
pp. 44–49
Photography: Courtesy of XRANGE/Kuo-Min Lee (pp. 44–45, 47, 48) & Lorenzo Pierucci Studio (pp. 46, 49)
Project Team: Grace Cheung, Royce Hong, Emily Lin, Peihsuan Hsu, Jason Chen, Miriam Park, Sonia Pan, Beatrice Cordella, Edgar Navarrete

ZAV ARCHITECTS
ZAVARCHITECTS.COM

Presence In Hormuz
pp. 62–65
Photography: Courtesy of ZAV Architects/Tahmineh Monzavi/instagram.com/tahminehmonzavi (pp. 62-63, 65 top & bottom right), DJI (p. 64), Soroush Majidi/instagram.com/soroushmajidi (p. 65 bottom left)
Lead Architects: Mohamadreza Ghodousi, Fatemeh Rezaei, Golnaz Bahrami, Soroush Majidi
Design Assistants: Sheila Ehsaei, Sara Jafari, Payman Barkhordari, Mohsen Safshekan, Kaveh Rashidzadeh, Hossein Panjehpour
Landscape: Maryam Yousefi, Morteza Adib
Interior Design: Sara Jafari, Taraneh Behboud, Sara Nikkar, Mohsen Dehghan

The ArchDaily Guide to Good Architecture

This book was conceived and edited by gestalten and ArchDaily.

Design and layout by gestalten
in cooperation with ArchDaily.

Edited by Robert Klanten, Daisy Woodward, and Rosie Flanagan
Contributing editor: ArchDaily

Foreword by Alejandro Aravena
Introduction by David Basulto

Feature texts by ArchDaily (Romullo Baratto: pp. 252–255, José Tomás Franco: pp. 150–153, Christele Harrouk: pp. 130–133, Dima Stouhi: pp. 282–285, and Nicolás Valencia: pp. 194–197)

Profile texts by Crystal Bennes (pp. 154–161, 172–179, 274–281) and Emily Burroughs (pp. 76–83, 304–311)

Chapter introductions by ArchDaily (Hana Abdel Latif: pp. 14–15, Mónica Arellano: pp. 102–103, 166–167, Claire Brodka: pp. 134–135, Fabián Dejtiar: pp. 224–225, Eduardo Leite Souza: pp. 290–291, Clara Ott: pp. 38–39, 256–257, Paula Pintos: pp. 66–67, Nicolás Valencia: pp. 198–199)

Project texts by Ruby Goss

Translation from Spanish: Alayne Pullen in association with First Edition Translations Ltd, Cambridge, UK (pp. 150–153, 194–197)
Translation from Portuguese: Maisie Musgrave in association with First Edition Translations Ltd, Cambridge, UK (pp. 252–255)

Editorial Management by Lars Pietzschmann for gestalten and Nicolás Valencia for ArchDaily

Cover, design, and layout by Stefan Morgner

Photo Editor: Madeline Dudley-Yates

Portrait illustrations by Oriana Fenwick

Typefaces: Everett by Nolan Paparelli and Aperçu by Colophon Foundry

Cover photography by Vincent Hecht
Back cover photography by ZAV Architects

Printed by Gutenberg Beuys Feindruckerei GmbH, Langenhagen
Made in Germany

Published by gestalten, Berlin 2022
ISBN 978-3-96704-064-7
ISBN 978-3-96704-078-4 (Special Edition)

For more information, and to order books, please visit www.gestalten.com

Bibliographic information published by the Deutsche Nationalbibliothek. The Deutsche Nationalbibliothek lists this publication in the Deutsche Nationalbibliografie; detailed bibliographic data is available online at www.dnb.de

None of the content in this book was published in exchange for payment by commercial parties or designers; gestalten selected all included work based solely on its artistic merit.

This book was printed on paper certified according to the standards of the FSC®.

MIX
Paper from responsible sources
FSC® C009051